Urban Housing Markets and Residential Location

Urban Housing Markets and Residential Location

Henry O. Pollakowski
Joint Center for Urban Studies
of MIT and Harvard University

LexingtonBooks
D.C. Heath and Company
Lexington, Massachusetts
Toronto

Library of Congress Cataloging in Publication Data

Pollakowski, Henry O.
  Urban housing markets and residential location.

  Includes bibliographical references and index.
  1. Residential mobility—United States—Mathematical models.
2. Municipal services—United States—Mathematical models. I. Title.
HD7288.92.U6P64   381'.456908'0973   78–20609
ISBN 0–669–02773–1   AACR2

Published simultaneously in Canada

Printed in the United States of America

International Standard Book Number: 0–669–02773–1

Library of Congress Catalog Card Number: 78–20609

To my parents

Contents

Contents

List of Figures
and Tables

Preface

This book presents applications of econometric methods to the study of urban housing markets and residential-location decisions. I have greatly benefited from numerous individuals' advice, suggestions, and assistance. I especially wish to thank George Break, Gardner Brown, Jr., Robert Halvorsen, Daniel McFadden, William Moss, Earl Rolph, and Thomas Rothenberg. Suresh Malhotra and Gerald Glandon conscientiously provided much of the computational assistance required. Gary Reid made numerous substantive and editorial contributions to the final version of the manuscript. Elisa Lusetti cheerfully and competently typed the final manuscript.

This work was supported primarily by National Institutes of Health research grants #1 R01 HD07410-01, -02, -03 from the National Institute of Child Health and Human Development, Center for Population Research. Additional support was received from a dissertation grant from the National Science Foundation and from awards by the University of Washington Graduate School Research Fund and the U.S. Department of the Interior. The Joint Center for Urban Studies of MIT and Harvard University provided support for the preparation of the final manuscript.

Chapters 1 and 2 consist of an extensive revision of material from my Ph.D. dissertation, "The Effects of Local Public Services on Residential Location Decisions: An Empirical Study for the San Francisco Bay Area" (Department of Economics, University of California at Berkeley, 1973). Chapter 3 is based on material previously published with Gardner M. Brown, Jr., and chapter 4 and appendix A are based on material published with Robert Halvorsen. I would like to thank both of these colleagues for their help and for their permission to use this material.

Introduction

The application of economic theory and econometrics to urban housing markets and residential location during the past decade has made a systematic study of numerous issues in urban economics possible for the first time. Practical applications of the concept of housing as a bundle of attributes and attempts to model residential choice in a nonmonocentric city are but two examples of this radical departure in the empirical literature.

The work presented in this book is part of this empirical literature. It exemplifies many of the themes of recent work on urban housing markets and residential location and makes original contributions both in areas that have not yet been studied and in areas that have been much studied but with different emphases. Methodology and careful use of microdata bases are emphasized in the hope that this will contribute to the quality of future studies.

Several themes are central to this book. One is the application of the concept of housing as a bundle of attributes, including not only structural attributes but also the location-specific attributes of neighborhood amenities, accessibility, and local public services. Another theme is the value of using large cross-section microdata sets for housing to examine a wide range of urban issues. Both a home interview survey and housing-sales data are employed for this purpose. A third theme is the application of the concept that households reveal their preferences for location-specific attributes, such as local public services, through their locational decisions. This concept motivates looking to the urban housing market to learn more about household preferences for neighborhood amenities and local public services.

The book is divided into three parts. Part I employs hedonic price equations to examine the relationship between a variety of local public services and rental values among a large sample of individual households in the San Francisco Bay Area. Part II applies the same hedonic price equation approach to two quite diverse issues: the value of green belts around bodies of water as reflected in property values and the effects on housing values of recent abrupt shifts in energy prices. In Part III, a multinomial logit model is employed to examine the individual household's choice of residential location in a large metropolitan area.

The two chapters that constitute part I present an examination of the effects of differentials in the levels of provision of several public services on rental values and consider what can be inferred about residential choice and the Tiebout hypothesis from these results. Results are obtained for several housing submarkets by employing a large housing microdata set for the San Francisco Bay Area.

Considerable evidence is presented that is consistent with a weak version of the Tiebout hypothesis. At the levels of provision existing during the sample period, households placed a positive value on educational services. Interesting variations among submarkets in the value placed on educational services are also observed. Plausible relationships between the provision of parks and recreational services and rental values are obtained in several cases; unfortunately, these estimates are imprecise. Evidence of the importance of fire protection is obtained in two of the six cases considered, and the magnitude of the effect of fire protection on rental values is plausible.

Part II presents applications of hedonic price equations for housing to two diverse issues. Chapter 3 presents a model of the determination of optimal water-related open space and estimates the relationship between property values and open space in order to learn the value of open space and to determine the optimal amount. This type of work is particularly important because shoreline development and use is a growing public policy issue in many urban areas. Furthermore, economists have not yet turned their attention to the economic significance of the existence and width of the undeveloped apron that offers public access to bodies of water in urban areas. Among the important issues that need to be considered here are whether we may expect the urban land market to provide a Pareto-efficient solution and whether public agencies, through zoning and other building restrictions, are acting in a socially optimal way. Chapter 3 begins an examination of these issues and presents empirical results employing microdata for Seattle, Washington.

The results indicate that the effect of variation in the width of the greenbelt surrounding a body of water is substantial. After a conceptual framework is developed to examine optimal width of such a greenbelt, some illustrative calculations are presented. Finally, the implications of the public-good characteristics of water-related open space are examined.

Chapter 4 uses a simple theoretical model to examine the relationship between fuel prices and house prices. It is shown that the magnitude of the effect on house prices of a given change in fuel prices is a function of the elasticity of demand for heating fuel, the expenditure on heating fuel, and the effect of changes in current fuel prices on expectations of future fuel prices. Thus, the magnitude of the effect on house prices of the changes in fuel prices that have occurred since the 1973 oil embargo is not obvious *a priori*. Empirical estimates of these effects indicate that fuel-price changes have resulted in significant changes in house prices, with lags of variable length between the changes in fuel prices and the corresponding changes in house prices.

Part III presents a model of the choice of residential location in a large metropolitan area. Employing extensive microdata for the San Francisco Bay Area, this model is estimated for households whose primary worker works in the San Francisco central business district. In choosing a residential location, a household is making decisions along several dimensions: tenure, location, structure type, and neighborhood and community type. The theoretical analysis of chapter 5 considers some of the difficult conceptual and empirical problems that arise in attempting to model this multidimensional choice. After examining some of these issues in the context of reviewing several related econometric studies, chapter 5 presents the locational-choice component of a general decision model of intrametropolitan residential choice.

The empirical results presented in chapter 6 underscore the importance of relative housing prices, search costs, and expected search or moving costs to the residential-location decision. Results such as these can provide useful information for considering how certain public policies or demographic changes might affect the residential-location choices of particular types of households and the pattern of those choices within an urban area. For example, results such as those presented here can be used to predict the effects of income changes brought about by changes in taxation or income-subsidy schemes and to examine how these responses vary across different types of households. Effects of changes in commuting costs brought about by increased gasoline prices, by taxes on automobile travel, or by construction of a new freeway or a rapid-transit system that reduces commuting time could also be examined with a model of this type. In these examples and in others, economic theory predicts responses to such changes that vary across households, and other empirical results can be used to test these implications.

**Part I
Local Public Services and
Housing Rental Values**

1

Background and
Theoretical Framework

In his seminal article, Charles Tiebout (1956) posited a world in which households reveal their demands for local public goods through their residential location decisions. Because households "vote with their feet" in a spatial setting, Tiebout argued, there is a much better chance that an optimal level of public good provision will be attained at the local level than at the national level. Beginning with the work of Oates (1969), numerous studies of the relationship among local public services, property taxes, and property values have attempted to provide some empirical verification of the Tiebout hypothesis.

This chapter and the one that follows present an examination of the effects of differentials in the levels of provision of several public services on rental values and examine what can be inferred about residential choice and the Tiebout hypothesis from these results. While most related work has concentrated on the explanation of property values, the approach taken here is to look specifically at the decision to purchase housing services. Thus, gross rents rather than property values provide the focus of attention here. Local public services are viewed as attributes of the package of housing services, and their implicit prices are estimated by regressing actual or imputed gross rental values on the relevant housing attributes. The importance of approaching the problem in this manner needs to be stressed. In the absence of a system of perfect benefit taxation, it is essential to have a measure of the price that households are willing to pay to consume a given menu of public services. The estimated implicit prices perform this function and, in doing so, lead to some advantages in interpreting the empirical results.[1]

In recognition of the diversity existing in menus of local public services, several public services are considered. This is done in the spirit of Tiebout's world, in which different communities offer different packages and no single index can be used to rank the communities. It is also recognized that it is possible to identify distinct but interrelated submarkets in which households demand public services. Results are thus presented in chapter 2 for submarkets distinguished by community type, housing tenure, and socioeconomic neighborhood composition. This permits comparisons between owner-occupants and renters and between white-collar and blue-collar households.

3

The notion that the spatial nature of residential choice forces households to reveal their preferences for local public services is central to the work presented in this and the following chapter. This effort should not, however, be viewed as a test of the Tiebout hypothesis in the form originally proposed by Tiebout. Instead, a weak version of the Tiebout hypothesis, in which the violation of certain of Tiebout's assumptions is recognized, is considered here. That is, the purpose of the work presented here is to measure the responsiveness of households to differentials in the levels of public service provision in a world where the supply of communities is not perfectly elastic and where persistent fiscal differences stemming from differences in fiscal capacities and public service production functions exist among communities.

This chapter first discusses the relevant theoretical background and then examines the residential choice problem facing a household in a metropolitan area where local public services vary among communities. This provides important background for the next section, in which a model of the determination of rental values is developed.

Background

Charles Tiebout (1956) provides a model that relates household location to preferences for local public services. Tiebout addresses the conclusion of the public goods analysis of Samuelson (1954, 1955) and Musgrave (1938, 1959)—that no market-type solution exists to the problem of determining the level of expenditures on public goods. He presents a model that shows that this conclusion does not necessarily apply to local expenditures. His model, by including residential choice, provides a conceptual solution to the problem of determining the level of expenditures for local public goods. Because the selection of a residential location allows households to choose from a wide variety of local public expenditure packages, this solution reflects consumer preferences better than they can be reflected at the national level, where all households must consume the same package of public goods.

The basic mechanism of the Tiebout model is that a household bases its choice of a community in which to locate on its preferences for public services. The model is based on a rather restrictive set of seven assumptions:

1. Households are fully mobile.
2. They have full knowledge of revenue and expenditure differences among communities and react to these differences.
3. A large number of communities exists.
4. There are no restrictions caused by employment opportunities.

5. There are no external economies or diseconomies of public services.
6. Given a pattern of public services, an optimum (minimum average cost) community size exists. (This ensures finding a determinate number of communities.)
7. Communities seek to reach and maintain their optimum size.

Tiebout then demonstrates that, in the limit, the total demand of city managers for local public services will approximate the demand that households would reveal if they were forced to state their true preferences. "There is no way in which the consumer can avoid revealing his preferences in a spatial economy. Spatial mobility provides the local public-goods counterpart to the private market's shopping trip" (Tiebout, 1956, p. 422).

The substantial subsequent literature has primarily taken two approaches. One set of studies has focused on the efficiency properties of Tiebout-type models (see, for example, Epple and Zellenitz, 1981). A second set of studies examines the relationship between fiscal variables and property values and provides the relevant background to the work presented here.[2] The first of these studies—the one that sets the tone for most ensuing empirical studies—was that of Oates (1969). Oates posits a utility-maximizing consumer who weighs benefits (from local public services) against costs (his tax liability) in choosing a community in which to reside. If this is a reasonable approximation to reality, it may be expected that, ceteris paribus, net rents will vary positively with the quality of local government services and negatively with local taxes. Given an increase in local taxes that is used to expand local public services, net rents may either increase or decrease, depending on the evaluation of the marginal benefits and costs by consumers. Oates' purpose was to measure the strength of these relationships in an attempt to determine whether the Tiebout hypothesis is relevant to real-world behavior.

Employing data for fifty-three New Jersey communities, Oates sets out to measure the effects of local public budgets on residential property values (and hence on net rentals). He selects median dwelling value as his left-hand variable, regressing it on the property tax rate, the per-pupil educational expenditure, and a number of other variables that are intended to account for the other influences on property values. He finds a significant negative relationship between effective property tax rates and property values and a significant positive relationship between public school expenditure per pupil (his proxy for output of local government services) and property values. Recognizing that the tax and government expenditure variables may be correlated with the error term, he then employs two stage least squares as his estimation method, obtaining similar results. He thus concludes, for his sample of New Jersey residential communities, (1) that a significant portion of a change in the local property tax rate will be capitalized, and (2) that his results are consistent with Tiebout's model of choice of residential location in that, other things held equal (including tax rates), property values (and thus net rentals) vary positively with the quality of local public services.

Several problems arose out of Oates' use of this methodology. The use of a single public service variable does not recognize the diversity existing in menus of local public services and leads to difficulties in interpreting the results (Pollakowski 1973b). In response to this criticism, Oates (1973) revised his specification, adding a second local public service variable (per capita expenditure on services other than education). His new results indicated that both public service variables had positive and significant effects on property values. In the work presented in this chapter and the one that follows, this diversity of public service menus is addressed.

A problem also exists with Oates' use of two-stage least squares to deal with the simultaneity problem (Pollakowski 1973b). Several of the additional predetermined variables that he uses to derive his predicted tax and expenditure variables are inappropriate because they are also correlated with the error term. To use two-stage least squares in this case as an estimation method, one must find additional exogenous variables that are correlated with the tax and education variables but not with the error term. A substantial portion of the error term is probably accounted for by attributes of a community that we would expect to vary with the quality of public services and the willingness to pay for them. A number of Oates' additional predetermined variables are correlated with these very attributes.[3] Suppose, for example, that an air pollution variable has been omitted from the right-hand side of Oates' equation. Households with more education tend to locate in areas with low pollution levels. Years of schooling thus should not be used as an additional predetermined variable, since it will be correlated with the error term. It appears that Oates' use of several inappropriate additional predetermined variables is responsible for his two-stage least squares results being very similar to his (plausible) ordinary least squares results. In fact, when three of his suspect additional predetermined variables are removed from a modified version of Oates' equation, the key coefficient estimates become very implausible, and their estimated standard errors become very large (Pollakowski 1973b). The nature of the problem with which we are concerned makes the discovery of appropriate additional predetermined variables difficult; attention is given later to resolving these difficulties.

Another specification problem with Oates' equation was raised by King (1977). King points out that use of the property tax rate as the tax variable causes the effect of the tax on property values to be independent of the value of the dwelling. He thus replaces the tax rate variable by the property tax payment itself to correct this misspecification. In the work presented in this chapter and the one that follows, the property tax rate is scaled by a measure of dwelling size to deal with this specification problem.

Numerous other studies have examined the effects of local public services and property taxes on property values. King (1973, 1975) and Noto (1976) provide examples of carefully done studies of this type. Bloom, Ladd, and Yinger (forthcoming) and Noto (1981) survey numerous relevant studies. In general, these studies support the hypothesis that fiscal differentials across jurisdictions are capitalized into property values.

The interpretation of this general result has been further examined in a series of papers that have emphasized supply-side considerations. Hamilton (1976), Peterson (1972), Edel and Sclar (1974), and Epple, Zelenitz, and Visscher (1978) have argued that a literal version of the Tiebout hypothesis implies an absence of any capitalization of fiscal variables. Tiebout assumes a perfectly elastic supply of all community types. His world is thus one in which the market for local public services is cleared by migration alone (Peterson 1972). In this literal or strong version of the Tiebout hypothesis, there is perfect benefit taxation; that is, benefits from higher levels of local public service provision are offset by the increased taxes required to pay for them. In this long-run equilibrium situation, consumers simply pay tax prices that are competitive supply prices. Since no fiscal residuals exist, there are no capitalization effects and we would not expect to obtain the type of results for fiscal variables hypothesized by Oates and others. The results of Oates (1969, 1973) and others are thus inconsistent with Tiebout's version of the Tiebout hypothesis.

If the possibility of supply restrictions on communities is introduced, however, fiscal residuals can exist and capitalization effects are possible. As pointed out by Yinger (1980, 1981), increases in the supply of communities are constrained by the opportunity cost of converting land to residential use. Suppliers will engage in this conversion only until it ceases to be profitable. Once housing suppliers are in equilibrium, fiscal residuals that have not been bid away will be capitalized. Thus, in this weak version of the Tiebout hypothesis, fiscal residuals arising from differences in fiscal capacities and public service production functions can persist in a modified Tiebout equilibrium in which capitalization effects are likely. The model presented in this chapter is designed to provide a test of a weak version of the Tiebout hypothesis.

A Model of Local Public Services and Housing Rental Values

Consider the residential choice problem facing a typical utility-maximizing household in a metropolitan area. The approach taken here is to view any given housing unit in a metropolitan area as embodying a bundle of attributes: a certain amount of living space, a certain ease of accessibility to shopping facilities, and so forth. The decision to view housing in this manner, an adaptation of Lancaster's (1966, 1971) work in consumer theory and

Rosen's (1974) work on implicit markets for attributes, is especially helpful in facilitating examination of the role played by public services. Public services may thus be viewed as attributes of the bundle of housing services, and the implicit prices of these public services in any given submarket may be examined.

Assume that, at a given point in time, a given distribution over space exists of the supplies of these attributes. This reflects the fact that the stock of housing is only altered slowly over time and that some attributes, such as certain neighborhood amenities, are absolutely limited in supply.

For a utility-maximizing household, these dwelling unit attributes will appear, along with other items, as arguments in its utility function. Taking the location of employment of the household worker as given, envision this household as maximizing its utility subject to the budget constraint that the total of its expenditure on housing services, its expenditure on other goods, and its commuting costs does not exceed its income.[4] Thus, for a given distribution of preferences and income and a given spatial distribution of employment, there exists a distribution of demands for attributes over space.[5] Since both supply and demand for housing attributes vary over space, the vector of implicit prices also varies. A metropolitan area is thus envisioned as consisting of a number of interrelated submarkets for housing attributes, including, of course, local public services.

To examine implicit attribute prices in a number of these submarkets, assume that, for any given submarket, the relationship among gross rental (actual or imputed) value (R_G), the quantities of dwelling unit attributes (q_i), and the implicit prices of dwelling unit attributes (r_i) is as follows:[6]

$$R_G = \sum_{i=1}^{k} r_i q_i \tag{1.1}$$

Estimates may thus be obtained of the vector of implicit prices by regressing actual or imputed value of dwelling units on the set of variables representing the attributes that we postulate are embodied in the dwelling unit.

Four types of dwelling unit attributes are considered, as follows:

$$R_G = \sum_{i} r_{1i} q_{1i} + \sum_{j} r_{2j} q_{2j} + \sum_{k} r_{3k} q_{3k} + \sum_{m} r_{4m} q_{4m} \tag{1.2}$$

where R_G is the gross rental (actual or imputed) of the dwelling unit; q_{1i} is the ith variable, representing structure; q_{2j} is the jth variable, representing neighborhood; q_{3k} is the kth accessibility variable; and q_{4m} is the mth public service variable.

In addition, one further right-hand variable must be included—the effective local property tax rate (TAXRT: the nominal rate adjusted by the relevant assessment ratio). If property tax rate differentials are fully capitalized into property values, there will be no relationship between effective property tax rates and standardized gross rentals. To the extent that this is not the case, however, omitting the tax variable means leaving out a determinant of rental differentials, thus biasing the coefficients of the variables correlated with it.

Several additional important relationships must also be considered. The levels of public service provision and tax rates not only affect rental values but are in turn affected by the wealth level of the community, which, in the case of primarily residential communities, is reflected in rental values. In addition, it is likely that levels of public service provision and tax rates are related to the nonresidential tax base, local non-property tax revenue, intergovernmental revenue, and differences in public service production functions. Equation 1.2 is thus most appropriately viewed as a member of a simultaneous system containing the following additional equations (assuming three public service variables):

$$q_{41} = g(\text{RTL}, \text{REV}_k, \text{COST}_e, \text{DEM}_f) \qquad (1.3)$$

$$q_{42} = h(\text{RTL}, \text{REV}_k, \text{COST}_e, \text{DEM}_f) \qquad (1.4)$$

$$q_{43} = k(\text{RTL}, \text{REV}_k, \text{COST}_e, \text{DEM}_f) \qquad (1.5)$$

$$\text{TAXRT} = m(\text{RTL}, \text{REV}_k, \text{COST}_e, \text{DEM}_f) \qquad (1.6)$$

where q_{4m} is the level of quality of public service m in a given community; RTL is the average rental value per period in the relevant community; REV_k is a set of revenue variables other than revenue from the property tax on local residential property; COST_e is a set of variables representing cost conditions in public service provision; DEM_f is a set of demographic variables; and TAXRT is the effective property tax rate. The choice of estimation method for the completely specified version of the model thus takes into consideration the existence of these relationships.

A number of considerations are important with respect to the choice of local public service variables. First, it is important to employ several variables to reflect the different market-clearing conditions for different local public services. In addition, use of a single proxy increases the likelihood of leaving out an important variable, thus biasing the coefficients of the variables correlated with it.

The relative importance of different public services in local budgets must also be considered. Table 1-1 indicates the relative levels of per capita expenditure in the thirty-eight largest SMSAs in the United States in 1964–1965. For the small, residential communities considered here, educa-

Table 1-1
Per Capita Expenditures of All Local Governments in the
Thirty-eight Largest SMSAs, 1964-1965

Category	Per Capita Expenditure
Education	$123.65
Highways	19.85
Public welfare	25.13
Health and hospitals	18.17
Police protection	17.27
Fire protection	9.87
Sewerage	10.20
Sanitation, other than sewerage	6.34
Parks and recreation	9.04
Water supply	15.34
Other utilities	19.22
Interest on general debt	11.54
General control	7.27
Other direct general expenditures	42.87

Source: U.S. Bureau of the Census, *Local Government Finances in Selected Metropolitan Areas in 1964-65,* Series GF-No. 9, 1966, table 1.

tional services account for an even greater portion of local government expenditure, since services such as public welfare and highways are much less important in these communities than they are in larger ones. In fact, educational services account for over one-half of local government expenditure in the communities considered in this study.

Finally, it is important that public services be employed for which there is a reasonable likelihood that households perceive differences across communities in levels of provision. Based on these considerations, three public services are employed: education, parks and recreation, and fire protection. Public welfare and highways were considered inappropriate for the reasonably small, residential communities considered in this study, while water supply, sewage disposal, refuse collection, other utilities, and general administration appear not to be perceived as varying substantially among the communities in the sample employed.

Use of a police variable as a public service variable was considered inadvisable. An important factor to households choosing a residential location is the perceived degree of safety in the proposed neighborhood. This factor, however, varies across the sample communities for a number of reasons, some most likely considerably more important than the quality of local police protection. It would be very difficult, however, to standardize adequately for these other factors in order to obtain an accurate measure of the influence of police quality on rental values. More specifically, consider the following extension of the simultaneous system of equations 1.2 through 1.6:

$$R_G = f(\text{CRIME}, \ldots) \qquad (1.2a)$$

$$\text{CRIME} = r(\text{DEM}_i, \text{PQUAL}) \qquad (1.7)$$

$$\text{PQUAL} = s(\text{DEM}_i, \text{POLINP}_j) \qquad (1.8)$$

$$\text{POLINP}_j = t(\text{RTL}, \text{REV}_k, \text{COST}_e, \text{DEM}_f) \qquad (1.9)$$

where CRIME is a variable representing the likelihood of a crime being committed during a given period of time in a given city; PQUAL is a measure of the quality of police protection in a given city; and POLINP_j is a set of variables representing the levels of various police inputs per period; and where it is anticipated that

$$\frac{\partial R}{\partial \text{CRIME}} < 0, \qquad \frac{\partial \text{CRIME}}{\partial \text{PQUAL}} < 0, \qquad \frac{\partial \text{PQUAL}}{\partial \text{POLINP}_j} > 0,$$

$$\frac{\partial \text{POLINP}_j}{\partial \text{RTL}} > 0, \qquad \frac{\partial \text{POLINP}_j}{\partial \text{REV}_i} > 0$$

Thus, the rental value of a given dwelling unit depends, among other things, on the likelihood of crime. The likelihood of crime, in turn, is a function of a number of demographic variables and the quality of police protection. In equation 1.8, the production function for police protection is specified, with police quality determined by a number of police inputs and by service conditions, which may be represented by a number of demographic variables. Finally, the levels of provision of various inputs are determined by the same types of considerations that determine the levels of output of the public services in equations 1.3 through 1.5.

Ideally, one would like to estimate this system of equations. Then the effect of police quality on rental values could be ascertained by multiplying the coefficient estimate of the CRIME variable in equation 1.2a by the coefficient estimate of the PQUAL variable in equation 1.7. Similarly, the effect of any given police input could be measured by multiplying the coefficient of the POLINP variable in equation 1.8 by the product just obtained. Unfortunately, adequate data are not available for the sample region, and estimation of this system is not attempted. Instead, a CRIME variable is used as one of the measures of neighborhood quality. If a significant negative coefficient is obtained for the CRIME variable, the most one can do is to combine that information with *a priori* beliefs about the magnitudes of the coefficients in the other (unestimated) equations. Of course, if the CRIME coefficient is not significantly different from zero, then, if there is no specification error, one can make a stronger statement about the absence of effects of police protection on rental values.

A linear functional form is employed for the basic rental equation 1.2. This formulation has the merit of simplicity, since the coefficients have the straightforward interpretation of implicit prices of units of attributes. It should be remembered, however, that this framework constrains the slope coefficient β_i to a single value for all values of the variables under consideration, $\partial^2 R/\partial X_i^2 = 0$. In addition, this framework embodies the assumption $\partial^2 R/\partial X_i X_j = 0$. In other words, the effect of any right-hand variable on the left-hand variable is independent of the other right-hand variables. This assumption is clearly not ideal, since it may be argued that some variables have a larger effect on larger dwelling units than on smaller ones. However, it is more likely that the public service variables have an equal absolute effect on the rentals of different size dwelling units, not an equal proportional effect, as would be implied by a multiplicative functional form. Of course, when using a linear functional form, individual variables can be altered when there is good reason to believe that an important nonlinearity exists. It was decided that such an alteration was in order for the tax variable, since the possibility existed of an important nonlinearity with respect to the relationship between the effective property tax rate and rental values. In a world where property tax changes are fully capitalized, we would expect a given change in the effective property tax rate to have a greater absolute effect on the value of a higher-valued dwelling unit than on the value of a dwelling unit with a lower market value. To the extent that this is not the case and that property tax differentials are reflected in gross rental values, we would also expect a nonlinear relationship to exist between effective property rates and gross rental values. In order to adjust roughly for this nonlinearity, TRTNRMS = (TAXRT) * (NROOMS) is employed as the tax variable instead of TAXRT.

Future work in this area can certainly benefit from further consideration of choice of functional form. Appendix A presents a general framework for choosing a functional form.

Concluding Comments

This chapter has raised a number of substantive and methodological issues that dictate the details of the empirical models estimated in the following chapter and the interpretation of their results. With respect to methodology, the empirical models reflect three important considerations. First, gross rental values rather than property values provide the focus of attention. This reflects an emphasis on examining the decision to purchase housing services and leads to certain advantages in interpreting the empirical results. Second, local public services are viewed as attributes of a multidimensional bundle of housing services, setting the stage for estimation of implicit prices of these services. Third, the heterogeneity of local public service bundles is recognized by including measures of three distinct services—education, parks and recreation, and fire protection—plus a closely related neighborhood variable in the empirical models of housing rental value.

On the substantive side, the models estimated in the following chapter provide a test of a weak version of the Tiebout hypothesis: that is, evidence is provided concerning how much value households place on local publicly provided services and, hence, whether households are likely to be responsive to public service differentials in choosing a residential location.

Notes

1. The only study employing gross rental values of which the author is aware is Sonstelie and Portney (1980).

2. See Oates (1981) for a discussion of numerous important aspects of the Tiebout literature.

3. The additional predetermined variables used by Oates were the median number of years of school completed by males of age twenty-five or older, the population density, the percentage of owner-occupied dwellings, the percentage of the population enrolled in public elementary and secondary schools, a dummy variable with the value of one for communities in Hudson County and a value of zero for municipalities in other counties, the value of commercial and industrial property per resident, and the percentage of change in population from 1950 to 1960.

4. We are, of course, assuming a very large menu of available combinations of housing attributes. Strictly speaking, since each household chooses a single dwelling unit, the budget set consists only of the points in attribute space that represent the combinations of housing attributes available. The optimal choice for a given household, therefore, will be found where an extreme point of the budget set touches the highest possible indifference surface. If we connect these extreme points of the budget set, we may view them as vertices occurring either at the intersection of facets or at the end of the efficiency frontier. Since the indifference surface cannot cut any of the facets that intersect at the optimum point, it follows that the slope in any direction of a plane tangent to the indifference surface at the

optimum point is bounded by the slopes, in the same direction, of the relevant facets. Thus, strictly speaking, the marginal rate of substitution between any two housing attributes will be bounded by the relevant ratios of their implicit prices. See Lancaster (1971, pp. 43–45).

5. See Rosen (1974) for a fuller discussion of this point.

6. One set of conditions under which this is strictly true is the following. Assume that the markets for units of housing services and for dwelling unit attributes are perfectly competitive and that costs are constant in the production of attributes. Also assume that the production function for units of housing services,

$$Q = f(q_1, q_2, \ldots, q_k)$$

is homothetic. Since we are thus assuming constant returns to scale, we may employ Euler's Law as follows:

$$Q = \frac{\partial Q}{\partial q_1} q_1 + \frac{\partial Q}{\partial q_2} q_2 + \ldots + \frac{\partial Q}{\partial q_k} q_k$$

where $\partial Q / \partial q_i$ is the marginal product of q_i. Since

$$\frac{\partial Q}{\partial q_i} = \frac{r_i}{P}$$

where P is the unit price of housing services, we can write

$$Q = \frac{r_1 q_1}{P} + \frac{r_2 q_2}{P} + \ldots + \frac{r_k q_k}{P}$$

Multiplying by P, we obtain

$$R_G = PQ = \sum_{i=1}^{k} r_i q_i.$$

2

The Sample and the Empirical Results

This chapter describes the sample, discusses the stochastic specification of the model, and presents the empirical results. The individual dwelling unit data are drawn from a random sample of approximately 29,000 households collected in 1965 for the Bay Area Transportation Study Commission (BATSC). They have been supplemented by some census tract data and data on local government activities. In addition, in order to construct the gravity index of accessibility, two further sources of data are employed: a BATSC inventory of almost all employment in the Bay Area by census tract location and a time-distance matrix from the Bay Area Simulation Study (BASS).

The BATSC data are uniquely suited to estimating the model employed here. This data set includes data for both owner-occupied and rental housing, and, in the rental housing case, for different structure types. The large sample size both facilitates precise estimation and permits results to be obtained for different tenure-structure type combinations. The existence of measures of basic dwelling unit characteristics, along with identification of location by census tract, allows the construction of empirical models whose results are unlikely to be seriously biased by the omission of important determinants of the structural relationships that provide the focus of this analysis.

The Sample

The sample of dwelling units consists of BATSC units of three tenure-structure combinations located in nineteen small, primarily residential communities in the San Francisco Bay Area. The sample consists of 2,105 owner-occupied single-family dwelling units, 217 rental units located in structures with two to four units, and 277 rental units located in structures with five to nineteen units. The communities chosen were the primarily residential ones in either the San Francisco-Oakland or the San Jose Urbanized Areas with 1960 populations between 10,000 and 50,000. The cities are distributed among five Bay Area counties, as shown in table 2-1.

The use of a sample of small residential suburbs is especially helpful in measuring public service quality. The choice of operational measures of local public service quality is very difficult, since good output measures are

Table 2-1
Sample Cities, Listed by County

Alameda County	San Mateo County
Albany	Belmont
Fremont	Burlingame
Piedmont	Daly City
	Menlo Park
Contra Costa County	Millbrae
El Cerrito	Pacifica
San Pablo	Redwood City
	San Bruno
Marin County	
Mill Valley	Santa Clara County
San Anselmo	Campbell
	Los Altos
	Mountain View
	Saratoga

not available. Use of input measures, however, can lead to difficulties, since there are cost differences and variations in service conditions across communities. Thus, the choice of a set of communities with some important similarities permits more confidence that input measures will reflect quality differentials in a tolerably accurate way.

The population, employment, and housing characteristics of the nineteen communities from which the sample is drawn suggest that even though the sample communities are small and primarily residential, a good deal of diversity still remains. In fact, the full range of close-in residential communities is represented. The percentage of employed males in white-collar occupations, which gives a general idea of the socioeconomic distribution of the population, varies a good deal, indicating substantial diversity among the sample communities. Table 2-2 presents, for each city, the distribution of census tracts into three groups: (1) those in which 60 percent or more of the employed males are in white-collar occupations, (2) those in which 40 to 60 percent of the employed males are in white-collar occupations, and (3) those in which 60 percent or more of the employed males are in blue-collar occupations. Six of the communities contain census tracts in all three categories (white collar, mixed, and blue collar), eight contain census tracts in two categories, and only five are highly homogeneous in the sense that they contain census tracts in only one category.

In most of the communities, the dwelling units are primarily owner-occupied, although in Albany, San Pablo, Burlingame, Menlo Park, and Mountain View less than 70 percent (but more than 55 percent) of the dwelling units are owner-occupied. The median number of persons per dwelling ranges from 2.8 in Mountain View, where there is a relatively large percen-

Table 2–2
Distribution of the Sample Census Tracts, by Composition of
Male Occupations

City	Number of Census Tracts		
	60 Percent or More White-Collar	Mixed	60 Percent or More Blue-Collar
Alameda County			
Albany	1	3	1
Fremont	0	2	4
Piedmont	2	0	0
Contra Costa County			
El Cerrito	2	2	3
San Pablo	0	0	4
Marin County			
Mill Valley	3	0	0
San Anselmo	2	1	0
San Mateo County			
Belmont	3	1	0
Burlingame	3	3	0
Daly City	4	0	4
Menlo Park	6	0	2
Millbrae	3	0	1
Pacifica	0	0	3
Redwood City	2	4	5
San Bruno	1	2	2
Santa Clara County			
Campbell	1	2	2
Los Altos	6	0	0
Mt. View	2	5	2
Saratoga	2	2	0
Total	43	27	33

Source: U.S. Bureau of the Census, *Census of Population, 1960,* 1963.

Note: The white-collar occupations consist of professional, technical, and kindred; managers, officals, and proprietors; clerical and kindred; and sales. The blue-collar occupations consist of craftsmen, foremen, and kindred; operatives; private household workers; service workers; and laborers.

tage of rental units, to 3.9 in Fremont. Most of the dwelling units in the sample communities are sound, with all plumbing facilities, although in San Pablo, San Anselmo, and Campbell less than 90 percent of dwellings are sound, with all plumbing facilities.[1]

The representativeness of the sample can be checked by comparing the sample with the housing stock as reported in the U.S. *Census of Housing.* Since this is a decennial census, the 1965 sample is compared with both the 1960 and the 1970 census counts. One such comparison is presented in table

Table 2-3
Distribution of Values of Owner-Occupied Single-Family Dwelling Units

	Percentage of Total[a]		
Market Value		BATSC Sample	
($000)	1960 Census	1965	1970 Census
0–5	0.4	0.3	0.1
5–10	4.0	0.5	0.5
10–15	21.7	2.8	2.0
15–20	34.6	15.0	8.4
20–25	19.2	25.2	20.6
25–35		32.4	36.1
35–50	} 20.1	17.3	20.2
50+		6.4	12.0

Sources: U.S. Bureau of the Census, *Census of Housing, 1960*, 1963; Bay Area Transportation Study Commission, 1965; U.S. Bureau of the Census, *Census of Housing, 1970*, 1973.
[a]Percentages may not add up to 100 because of rounding.

2-3, which compares the percentage distributions of values of owner-occupied single-family dwelling units in the nineteen sample communities for the 1960 census, the 1970 census, and the BATSC sample. Judging from this rough comparison, it appears that the sample is fairly representative with respect to market value categories, although two of the lower-valued categories ($5,000–$10,000 and $10,000–$15,000) may be somewhat under-represented.

Table 2-4 lists the variables and their sources. Imputed annual gross rental value (IMPRTL) for owner-occupied units is computed as follows:

$$R_G = R_N + M + D + T$$
$$= rV + sV + qV + tV$$
$$= (r + s + q + t)V$$

where R_N is the annual net rental; M is the annual maintenance expenditure; D is the annual depreciation; T is the annual property taxes paid; V is the market value of the property; r is the opportunity rate of return; s is the estimate of annual maintenance expenditure as a fraction of market value; q is the estimate of annual depreciation as fraction of market value; and t is the annual effective property tax rate.

An appropriate value of r for 1965 is about 5 percent; Aaron (1970) uses 4 percent and 6 percent for 1966. Most estimates of s indicate that it averages about 1 to 1.5 percent; see Shelton (1968) for a survey of these estimates. A value of s of 1.5 percent is thus used here. If we assume that

Table 2-4
Definitions and Sources of Variables

Variable	Definition	Source[a]
Left-hand variables:		
IMPRTL	Imputed annual rental value (owner-occupied units)	(4, 5, 14)
RENT	Actual annual rental value (rental units)	(4)
Right-hand variables:		
Housing quality		
NROOMS	Number of rooms	(4)
LOTSIZ	Size of lot (in acres)	(4)
AGEDUM1	Age dummy: one if built before 1940; zero otherwise	(4)
AGEDUM2	Age dummy: one if built 1940–1949; zero otherwise	(4)
AGEDUM3	Age dummy: one if built 1950–1959; zero otherwise	(4)
Neighborhood quality		
MEDRMS	Median number of rooms per dwelling unit in relevant census tract	(22)
DENSITY	Percentage of dwelling units in relevant census tract with more than one person per room	(22)
GOLF	Special feature dummy: one if relevant census tract contains a special feature, such as a golf course or an institution with spacious, well-landscaped grounds; zero otherwise	(11)
MOUNTS	Terrain and view dummy: one if census tract is in or contiguous to rolling terrain; zero otherwise	(11)
CRIME	Felony crime rate for relevant city	(9)
Accessibility		
JOBACC	Gravity index of accessibility to all employment in the Bay Area	(2, 3)
Public services		
EDUEXP	Current public educational expenditure per pupil in relevant city	(1, 7, 8, 12, 13, 15, 17, 18, 19)
PARKEX	Per capita expenditure on parks and recreation in relevant city	(20,23)
FIRE	Number of fire stations per square mile in relevant city	(10, 16)
Tax variable		
TRTNRMS	Adjusted tax variable: (TAXRT)(NROOMS), where TAXRT is the nominal total property tax rate adjusted by the relevant assessment ratio (mean of the three fiscal years (1962–1963 to 1964–1965)	(4, 5, 14)

[a]Data sources are as follows:
(1) Alameda County Superintendent of Schools, *Grade by Grade Enrollment Summary as of the End of the First School Month, 1965-66,* Business Services Bulletin No. 12, Hayward, November 1965.
(2) Bay Area Simulation Study, 1968.
(3) Bay Area Transportation Study Commission, *Employment Inventory, 1964.*
(4) Bay Area Transportation Study Commission, *Household Survey,* 1965.
(5) California State Controller, *Annual Report of Equalization,* Sacramento, 1964–1966.
(6) California State Controller, *Annual Report of Financial Transactions Concerning Cities of California, Fiscal Year 1965-66,* Sacramento, 1967.
(7) California State Department of Education, *Enrollment in California Public Schools, Fall, 1965,* Sacramento, 1966.
(8) California State Department of Education, *The State School Fund and Educational Statistics for the Fiscal Year Ending June 30, 1967,* Parts I and III, Sacramento, 1967.

Table 2–4 continued

(8) California State Department of Education, *The State School Fund and Educational Statistics for the Fiscal Year Ending June 30, 1967,* Parts I and III, Sacramento, 1967.

(9) California State Department of Justice, *Crime and Delinquency in California, 1965,* Sacramento.

(10) California State Deparment of Public Works. *Population, Area, and Concentration in the Incorporated Cities of California, as of January 1, 1965,* Sacramento.

(11) Constructed by author for 1965.

(12) Contra Costa County Department of Education, *Elementary and Secondary Enrollment by District in Contra Costa County—October 1965,* Pleasant Hill, November 1965.

(13) Information supplied by local school districts.

(14) Information supplied by tax collector's offices, counties of Alameda, Contra Costa, Marin, San Mateo, and Santa Clara.

(15) Marin County Superintendent of Schools, *Enrollment—End of the Sixth School Month: 1965–66,* Statistical Bulletin No. 1, Corte Madera, April 1966.

(16) O. Nolting and D. Arnold. eds., *The Municipal Year Book, 1966,* vol. 33, Chicago, 1966.

(17) San Mateo County Department of Education, *Comparison of Enrollment by Types: October 1965 and October 1966,* Statistical Bulletin No. 7A, Redwood City, November 1966.

(18) San Mateo County Department of Education, *Male and Female Enrollment as of October, 1966,* Statistical Bulletin No. 7B, Redwood City, November 1966.

(19) Santa Clara County Office of Education, *Active Enrollment as of End of Sixth School Month, Spring 1966,* San Jose.

(20) State of California, *The California Cities: Comparative Expenditures and Expenditure Patterns by Urbanized and Non-Urbanized Areas, 1966–67,* Sacramento, 1968.

(21) U.S. Bureau of the Census, *Census of Business, 1967,* Washington, 1970.

(22) U.S. Bureau of the Census, *Census of Housing, 1960,* Washington, 1963.

(23) U.S. Bureau of the Census, *Census of Population, 1960,* Washington, 1963.

land will not fall in value and that land makes up one-fourth of the original property value, then, for a building with a useful life of fifty years, the annual cost of obsolescence is about 1.5 percent. Thus, a value of q of 1.5 percent is used here. Since values of t are distributed about a median of about 2 percent, $(r + s + q + t)$ will be distributed about a median of 10 percent.

Data on owner's equity and interest payments are not available and thus are not used in determining imputed gross rental. This is not considered a serious problem, however, since it is reasonable to assume that the mortgage interest rate determines not the total rate of return on the housing, but only the division of the total rate of return between the occupant and the lender.

The BATSC survey provided data on property values only in interval ranges. For use in this study, each of these value ranges had to be converted to a single median figure. The interval medians used by BATSC for this purpose, which appeared quite reasonable, were adopted and are presented in table 2–5. Annual rental value (RENT) for rental units was obtained by multiplying the monthly figure obtained from the BATSC survey by 12.

The variables representing structure and land area are drawn from the BATSC survey. Number of rooms is employed as a measure of living space.

Table 2–5
Property Value Intervals and Medians
(dollars)

Value Interval	Median
Less than 5,000	2,500
5,000 to 9,999	7,500
10,000 to 14,999	12.500
15,000 to 19,999	17.500
20,000 to 24,999	22,500
25,000 to 29,999	27,500
30,000 to 34,999	32,500
35,000 to 39,999	37,500
40,000 to 44,999	42,500
45,000 to 49,999	47,500
50,000 to 54,999	52,500
55,000 to 59,999	57,500
60,000 and over	75,000

An alternative and complementary measure, square feet of living space, was not available. Lot size was available from the BATSC survey in interval ranges. The intervals and the interval medians used here are presented in table 2-6. Structure age data were available in four interval ranges. For each of the periods pre-1940, 1940-1949, and 1950-1959, a dummy variable with the value of 1 if the dwelling unit was built during the relevant period, zero otherwise is constructed. The period 1960-1965 is used as *numeraire*.

The neighborhood variables selected consist mostly of census tract measures. For a general quality proxy, the median number of rooms per dwelling unit in the relevant census tract was selected. As a measure of crowding, a density variable was chosen: the percentage of dwelling units in the relevant census tract with more than one person per room. Numerous neighborhoods in the sample area are located either in or contiguous to rolling terrain. A dummy variable was thus constructed, with a value of 1 if the relevant census tract was in one of these areas, zero otherwise. It was also thought that special green areas are valued by prospective and current residents of an area, and a dummy variable was thus constructed with a value of 1 if the relevant census tract contained a golf course, an institution with spacious, well-landscaped grounds, or a similar feature, and a value of zero otherwise. As discussed earlier, use of a neighborhood measure of perceived safety is preferable to use of a police public service variable. The felony crime rate in the relevant city is thus included.

The unique geographical features of the sample region make the measurement of locational advantage difficult. There are three major downtown areas and a number of scattered smaller centers of activity, and the shape of San Francisco Bay determines accessibility patterns to a significant degree. Given these considerations, a gravity index of accessibility to

Table 2–6
Lot Size Intervals and Medians
(acres)

Lot Size Interval	Median
Less than 0.1	0.075
0.1 to 0.2	0.15
0.2 to 0.3	0.25
0.3 to 0.5	0.40
0.5 to 1.0	0.70
1.0 or more	1.25

all employment in the Bay Area is employed as the index of accessibility. Each census tract is assigned an index value equal to

$$\sum_j \frac{E_j}{(d_j)^2}$$

where E_j is total employment in the jth census tract, d_j is freeflow driving time from the census tract in question to the jth census tract, and the summation is done over all census tracts except the one in question. The index was truncated at 45 minutes, since it is reasonable to assume that the existence of employment opportunities located more than 45 minutes from a dwelling unit would not appreciably affect the rental value of the unit. Appendix B presents the values of this index for each census tract, along with a more detailed description of the data employed.

Current educational expenditure per pupil is used to measure educational output. Perceived educational benefits are probably highly correlated with expenditure per pupil, even if expenditure is not a strong determinant of level of achievement in terms of test scores. Perceived benefits, after all, are the important factor with respect to household location decisions. Capital costs are excluded from this measure. Debt service varies a good deal among districts of different age, and it is inappropriate to consider the newer districts as producing higher quality educational services simply because their buildings have been built more recently. Differences among communities in financing public capital expenditures are not considered. Other measures were considered but rejected for various reasons. Scores on standardized tests are not employed because they are influenced by nonschool factors, such as home environment. Similarly, the number of high school graduates accepted at a four-year college reflects a good deal more than educational quality. Average class size, though it has conceptual merit, is not employed because of data difficulties.

The local government variables are defined at the citywide level. It was necessary to construct the variable for current public educational expenditure per pupil for two reasons. First, since education cost is greater at higher grade levels, a weighted average of enrollments had to be employed. Second, the data on expenditure and enrollment are available not by city but by elementary and secondary school districts. Typically, a city contains one or more elementary school districts, while high school districts usually coincide with a number of elementary districts. Since high school districts often contain portions of more than one city, adjustments had to be made in order to obtain per-pupil expenditure by city. The procedure adopted here was to impute the enrollment and expenditures of a high school district to the various elementary school districts that coincide with it. The algorithm employed to construct the educational expenditure per pupil variable is presented in appendix C. The data employed are listed in table 2-4.

Parks and recreational facilities arc a local public good that is impure because of nonsymmetry in consumption (benefits declining with distance from the site of provision) and partial rivalry in consumption (congestion). An ideal measure would thus take account of not only the quality of the services at its site of provision (for example, the size and intensity of development of a park) but also the distance from the dwelling unit to the site and some measure of congestion (such as the population within some arbitrary distance of the site or an actual measure of use). Unfortunately, the nature of dwelling unit data does not allow this degree of fine tuning, and a less ideal measure is employed. Per capita expenditure on parks and recreation is thus employed as an output measure. This measure is more appropriate than total land area devoted to parks in the relevant city, which ignores intensity of development, and it is also more appropriate than expenditure per developed acre, which ignores the size and number of parks. A dummy variable for the presence of a park in the relevant census tract is not employed since it does not represent size and quality of the park. In addition, most tracts in the sample contain a park.

Fire protection also exhibits nonsymmetry in consumption and partial rivalry in consumption. As is the case with parks and recreation, the nature of the data does not permit construction of a variable based on, say, the distance to the nearest fire hydrant and the distance to the nearest fire station. The number of fire stations per square mile in the relevant city is thus employed as a measure of perceived fire protection. A reasonable alternative course of action with respect to fire safety would be to use the underwriter's fire insurance rating of the city as a neighborhood quality variable.

The tax variable (TRTNRMS) is the product of TAXRT and NROOMS, where TAXRT is the nominal total property tax rate adjusted by the relevant assessment ratio. The mean of the three fiscal years 1962–

1963 to 1964–1965 is employed.[2] Table 2–7 presents the values of the local government variables for the sample cities.

In chapter 1 the assumption was made that a large menu of different dwelling units was available. It was assumed that, given its tastes, a household purchased a bundle of dwelling unit attributes (along with other goods and commuting) so that it maximized its utility subject to its budget constraint. Implicit in this formulation is the assumption that the household will indeed by able to find the bundle that it prefers at the prevailing implicit prices. If the preferred bundle is not available, the household will be forced to choose a suboptimal bundle, and its pattern of consumption thus will not represent its true preferences. This leads to the question of the likelihood that the preferred bundle is indeed available.

At the level of aggregation used in this study, it is reasonable to assume that households have found their preferred bundles. If owner-occupied single family dwelling units are grouped into five categories defined by number of rooms (four or fewer, five, six, seven, eight or more), almost 70 percent of the tracts in the sample provide dwelling unit size options in at least four of these five categories, while less than eleven percent provide two or fewer dwelling unit-size choices. It is evident that even at the census tract level, a good deal of choice exists with respect to dwelling unit size. Appendix D presents the distribution of owner-occupied single-family dwelling units by number of rooms by census tract.

If owner-occupied single-family dwelling units are cross-classified into three unit-size categories (five rooms or less, six to seven rooms, and eight or more rooms) and three lot size categories (less than 0.1 acres, 0.2–0.3 acres, and more than 0.3 acres), then households searching in these 103 census tracts faced on average 4.6 out of a maximum of 9 possible alternatives in each of these census tracts. Similarly, if these units are cross-classified by the same three unit-size categories and two structure-age categories (twenty-five years or older, less than twenty-five years old), then households faced, on average, almost 3.9 alternatives of a maximum possible of six per census tract. In short, even within census tracts the available combinations of unit size and lot size, as well as of unit size and structure age, are quite varied. Appendix E presents the distribution of owner-occupied single-family dwelling units by these two cross-classifications by census tract.

The simple correlations among the dwelling unit attributes are presented in appendix F. Their generally low values provide further evidence of the availability of varied combinations of dwelling unit attributes.

The Stochastic Specification of the Model

Two potential difficulties with the stochastic specification of the model must be considered: the possibility that the disturbance term of the stochas-

Table 2-7
Values of Local Public Service and Property Tax Variables

City	Educational Expenditure per Pupil (EDUEXP)	Fire Stations per Square Mile (FIRE)	Parks and Recreational Expenditure per Capita (PARKEX)	Effective Property Tax Rate (TAXRT)
Alameda County				
Albany	$514	0.58	$ 6.06	1.99%
Fremont	450	0.07	7.96	2.01
Piedmont	576	0.56	17.55	2.47
Contra Costa County				
El Cerrito	544	0.70	13.11	2.03
San Pablo	544	0.71	14.66	2.26
Marin County				
Mill Valley	574	0.32	14.51	2.25
San Anselmo	563	1.00	3.93	2.19
San Mateo County				
Belmont	568	0.61	3.35	1.92
Burlingame	658	0.79	11.38	1.68
Daly City	539	1.20	4.77	2.00
Menlo Park	669	0.62	7.36	2.00
Millbrae	637	0.31	3.15	1.80
Pacifica	487	0.26	6.76	2.09
Redwood City	605	0.14	8.27	1.97
San Bruno	614	0.55	7.34	1.86
Santa Clara County				
Campbell	466	0.47	0.99	2.13
Los Altos	568	0.52	6.79	2.08
Mountain View	579	0.34	11.26	2.12
Saratoga	501	0.44	0.99	1.90

Sources: See table 2–4.

tic form of equation 1.2 in chapter 1 is heteroscedastic and the possibility of a simultaneity problem. The first potential difficulty stems from the fact that the sample dwelling units vary in size and value. Since it is to be expected that observations on larger dwelling units have larger disturbance terms than do observations on smaller units, it is questionable whether the standard Gauss-Markov assumption of a scalar covariance matrix is a tolerable approximation to reality. Although this deficiency will not cause estimates to be biased, it will cause them to be inefficient. In order to obtain best linear unbiased estimates, the stochastic specification must be such that the assumption of a scalar covariance matrix can be made. Thus, in order to approach a homoscedastic specification, the observations corresponding to high variance are discounted. Choosing $\sigma^2 N^2$ (where N = NROOMS) as the specification of the variance of the disturbance term of the stochastic form of equation 1.2, all observations are thus weighted by $1/N$.

The second potential difficulty concerns the possibility of a simultaneity problem. As discussed earlier, the basic rental equation 1.2 is most appropriately viewed as part of the simultaneous equation system 1.2 through 1.6. If this is the case, the possibility that the local government variables are correlated with the disturbance term in the stochastic form of equation 1.2 must be considered. This will produce biased point estimates of the coefficients in the case where ordinary least squares is used as the method of estimation. More specifically, the possibility exists that a substantial portion of this disturbance term is accounted for by certain intangible attributes of a neighborhood or community, which we would expect to vary with the quality of public services and the willingness to pay for them. It is very difficult to find appropriate variables that reflect these intangible attributes. Although variables such as educational attainment or family income do reflect these intangible attributes, it is inappropriate to employ these variables as right-hand variables in the basic rental equation because they are attributes of the local population, not attributes of the package of housing services. This distinction is an important one: if the level of provision of a local public service changes, this change will affect the demographic composition of the community. Thus, if any demographic variables are employed as right-hand variables, the underlying *ceteris paribus* assumption will be violated. The three local public service variables and the local tax variable are thus treated as endogenous right-hand variables. In addition, since it was postulated in equation 1.7 of chapter 1 that the CRIME variable was a function not only of the quality of police services but of a number of local demographic variables, the CRIME variable is also treated as endogenous. Thus, treating these five variables as endogenous, two-stage least squares is employed in order to obtain estimates that are consistent and asymptotically efficient.

At least five additional predetermined variables that are believed to be correlated with the endogenous variables but not with the disturbance term must be employed. Care must be taken not to choose additional predetermined variables (such as family income) that are correlated with intangible attributes that, as just pointed out, make up a substantial portion of the disturbance term. The six variables employed and their data sources are presented in table 2–8.

Since the five endogenous right-hand variables are defined not at the individual dwelling unit level but at the citywide level, the use of two-stage least squares must be altered slightly. In the first stage, each of the five endogenous variables is regressed on all the exogenous variables in the system in order to obtain predicted values of the endogenous variables. Since these five endogenous variables are citywide, it is most appropriate to regress them on other citywide variables in the first stage. Thus, the six additional predetermined variables chosen for use are also defined at the citywide level. The exogenous right-hand variables in the basic rental equa-

Table 2–8
Additional Predetermined Variables Used in Two-Stage
Least Squares

Variable	Source
Commercial and industrial property value per resident[a]	U.S. Bureau of the Census, *Census of Housing, 1960* (1963); U.S. Bureau of the Census, *Census of Population, 1960,* (1963); Californial State Controller, *Annual Report of Financial Transactions Concerning Cities of California, Fiscal, Year 1965–66* (1967); California State Controller, *Annual Report of Equalization* (1966).
Total retail sales	U.S. Bureau of the Census, *Census of Business, 1967* (1970).
Local nonproperty tax	California State Controller, *Annual Report of Financial Transactions Concerning Cities of California, Fiscal Year 1965–66* (1967); U.S. Bureau of the Census, *Census of Population, 1960* (1963).
Intergovernmental revenue per resident	California State Controller, *Annual Report of Financial Transactions Concerning Cities of California, Fiscal Year 1965–66* (1967); U.S. Bureau of the Census, *Census of Population, 1960* (1963).
Percentage of school population in local public schools	U.S. Bureau of the Census, *Census of Population, 1960,* (1963).
Percentage of population enrolled in local schools	U.S. Bureau of the Census, *Census of Population, 1960* (1963).

[a]Since the market value of commercial and industrial property per resident was not available, it was estimated by

$$\frac{(e/f) - abd}{g}$$

where a is the total number of occupied housing units, b is the percentage of housing units that are owner-occupied, d is the median dwelling value, e is the total assessed value of all property, f is the equalization ratio, and g is population.

tion 1.2 are defined, however, either at the individual dwelling unit level or at the census tract level. Thus, in the first stage, citywide equivalents of these are employed. These equivalents, along with their sources or derivations, are listed in table 2 9.

Since the usual method of computing the variance-covariance matrix in the case of two-stage least squares cannot be employed here, the following procedure was employed to obtain a sum of squared residuals, a variance-

Table 2-9
Sources or Derivations of Citywide Equivalents of Exogenous Right-Hand Variables in Equation 1.2

Variable	Source or Derivation
Median number of rooms	U.S. Bureau of the Census, *Census of Housing, 1960* (1963)
Mean lot size[a]	Mean of the individual sample observations
Percentage of dwelling units built before 1950	U.S. Bureau of the Census, *Census of Housing, 1960* (1963)
Percentage of dwelling units with more than one person per room	U.S. Bureau of the Census, *Census of Housing, 1960* (1963)
Special feature variable (GOLF)	Percentage of census tracts that contain a special feature, such as a golf course or an institution with spacious, well-landscaped grounds
Terrain-and-view variable (MOUNTS)	Percentage of census tracts in or contiguous to rolling terrain
Accessibility	Mean of the census tract values of the gravity index of accessibility

[a]The mean lot size variable was not employed in the regressions for rental dwelling units since it was not specified as an exogenous variable in those cases.

covariance matrix, and hence the appropriate standard errors of regression coefficients. In computing the sum of squared residuals, the predicted values of the left-hand variable are obtained by multiplying the matrix of observations on the original right-hand variables by the vector of final (second-stage) regression coefficients. Having computed the sum of squared residuals, the standard error of the regression may be computed. Multiplying the square of this standard error by the matrix of right-hand variables employed in the second stage described above, the revised variance-covariance matrix and hence the revised standard errors of the estimated regression coefficients are obtained.

Empirical Results: An Overview

The empirical results consist of estimations of the basic rental equation 1.2 for various submarkets. First, results for the entire sample of single-family owner-occupied dwelling units are presented. Then results are presented for various subsamples that approximate important submarkets. Given the special interest here in the effects of educational services, the observations on dwelling units with four rooms or fewer were deleted under the assumption that they are outside the submarket of households containing school-age children. Then, in order to obtain some information about how evaluation of public services varies among segments of the metropolitan population, the owner-occupied sample was divided into two subsamples: those dwelling in predominantly white-collar census tracts and those in census tracts that are not predominantly white-collar.

A situation in which distinct socioeconomic groups demanded housing services in spatially separate markets would be ideal here, of course. Although neither completely distinct groups nor spatially segmented markets exist within the sample, it nevertheless can be argued that markets are segmented to a considerable degree and that useful subsamples can be drawn. The predominantly white-collar census tracts are those in which 60 percent or more of the males were in white-collar occupations. Data restrictions did not allow use to be made of corresponding predominantly blue-collar census tracts. Thus, results are presented for dwelling units in the census tracts that were not predominantly white-collar as just defined. For rental dwelling units, separate results are presented for two different structure types: dwelling units in structures containing two to four units and dwelling units in structures containing five to nineteen units.

The estimated implicit prices of local public services measure the dependence of rental values on levels of provision of public services. A positive public service coefficient tells us that, for a given supply of the service, demand is such that the market clears at a positive price; in other words, households place a positive value on the service and consider it in choosing their bundle of housing services, including location. Thus, a positive coefficient is consistent with a weak version of the Tiebout hypothesis. On the other hand, if households do not value marginal increases in a public service, a coefficient of zero will be obtained.

The interpretation of the local public service coefficients is more useful employing imputed gross rental value than property value as the left-hand variable. That is, as long as households place, at the margin, a positive value on a local public service, a positive public service coefficient estimate should be obtained. As discussed in chapter 1, however, in the case of a long-run no-capitalization equilibrium posited by Hamilton (1976) and others, use of property value as the left-hand variable implies that the relationship between property value and local public services hypothesized by Oates and others would not be found. As discussed earlier, the no-capitalization equilibrium is an unlikely case. Nevertheless, the economic forces underlying this argument may very well lead to a partial-capitalization equilibrium in which the advantage of employing gross rental value as the left-hand variable would remain. That is, the more closely local property taxes approach a system of perfect benefit taxation, the more difficult it would be to interpret the relationship between local taxes and services and individual property values.

Unfortunately, the sensitivity of households to variations in public service provision cannot be completely specified without estimating public service demand functions. In the case considered here, given the (fixed) supply of a public service at a point in time, knowledge of the implicit price gives us one point on the demand curve. While this is quite useful, it is important to recognize the limitations of this approach.

Results for Owner-Occupied Dwelling Units

The results for owner-occupied dwelling units are based on a sample of 2,105 single-family owner-occupied dwelling units for which data are available in the nineteen residential communities listed in table 2-1. Table 2-10 presents the means and standard deviations of the variables employed. Column I of table 2-11 presents the parameter estimates for this sample. As explained earlier, all observations are weighted by 1/NROOMS in order to approach a homoscedastic specification, and two-stage least squares is employed as an estimation method in view of the likelihood of a simultaneity problem.[3] All but two of the coefficient estimates are of the hypothesized signs, and the degree of precision of the estimates is generally high. The neighborhood variables appear to be important, and accessibility to jobs has a positive effect on rental values. The perceived safety variable and the tax variable do not have the expected signs, but the hypotheses that their respective coefficients are zero cannot be rejected at the .05 level of significance.[4]

To provide a test of the reasonableness of including the set of public service variables in an equation of this type, an F test is performed of the null hypothesis that the coefficients of the three public service variables are jointly equal to zero against the alternative that they are not.[5] This null hypothesis is rejected at the .005 level, making it highly unlikely that the true local government coefficients are jointly equal to zero.[6] The coefficient estimates of the three public service variables are each of the hypothesized sign. The hypothesis that the coefficient of EDUEXP is zero can be rejected at the .01 level, while the respective hypotheses that the coefficient of FIRE and PARKEX are zero cannot be rejected at the .05 level.[7]

Assuming an average of 1.5 pupils per single-family owner-occupied dwelling, an EDUEXP coefficient of .00150 would imply that an increase in educational expenditure sufficient to raise per-pupil expenditure one dollar would be fully reflected in rental values. The estimated coefficient of .00319

Table 2–10
Single-Family Owner-Occupied Dwelling Units: Means and Standard Deviations

Variable	Mean	Standard Deviation
IMPRTL	2.856	1.234
NROOMS	6.15	1.44
AGEDUM1	0.198	0.399
AGEDUM2	0.159	0.366
AGEDUM3	0.426	0.495
LOTSIZ	0.237	0.224
MEDRMS	5.26	0.57
DENSITY	7.03	5.97
GOLF	0.337	0.473
MOUNTS	0.437	0.496
CRIME	14.57	4.06
JOBACC	1.048	0.491
EDUEXP	548.0	64.5
FIRE	0.494	0.323
PARKEX	7.84	3.96
TRTNRMS	12.45	3.31

Note: See table 2-4 for definitions of these variables.

Table 2–11
Estimated Implicit Prices, Owner-Occupied Single-Family Dwelling Units

Variable	I (N = 2,105)	II (N = 1,991)
Constant	−2.47	−2.65
	(.343)	(.351)
Housing quality		
NROOMS	.318	.391
	(.0844)	(.0841)
LOTSIZ	2.00	2.16
	(.0839)	(.0971)
AGEDUM1 (25+ yrs.)	−.511	−.445
	(.0633)	(.0644)
AGEDUM2 (15–24 yrs.)	−.430	−.397
	(.0637)	(.0647)
AGEDUM3 (6–14 yrs.)	−.254	−.215
	(.0504)	(.0491)
Neighborhood quality		
MEDRMS	.253	.299
	(.0386)	(.0397)
DENSITY	−.0238	−.0212
	(.00388)	(.00388)
GOLF	.0911	.112
	(.0405)	(.0414)
MOUNTS	.103	.0913
	(.0413)	(.0418)

Table 2–11 continued

Variable	I (N = 2,105)	II (N = 1,991)
CRIME	.00466	−.00257
	(.00648)	(.00661)
Accessibility		
JOBACC	.112	.0865
	(.0536)	(.0560)
Public services		
EDUEXP	.00319	.00302
	(.000452)	(.000461)
PARKEX	.00228	.00312
	(.00659)	(.00676)
FIRE	.0528	.129
	(.0833)	(.0870)
Tax variable		
TRTNRMS	−.00336	−.0376
	(.0400)	(.03993)
SSR	38.82	33.11
SE	.137	.130

Column I: Total sample of owner-occupied single-family dwelling units.
Column II: Column I with small dwelling units (four rooms or fewer) removed.
Left-hand variable is imputed gross rental value, in thousands of dollars.
All observations are weighted by 1/NROOMS.

exceeds it by a fair (and statistically significant) amount, implying that a given increase in the provision of educational services would be valued at more than cost.

Although the fact that educational services have a substantial effect on rental values is more important than the exact magnitude of the relevant coefficient estimate, it is nevertheless important to consider the possible reasons for the degree to which the coefficient estimate exceeds the benchmark coefficient of .00150. One possibility is that certain intangible neighborhood attributes have not been specified adequately in the basic equation and are correlated with EDUEXP. If this were the case, EDUEXP would be partially representing these attributes. However, in earlier regression runs, additional neighborhood variables were employed and did not have the effect of lowering the EDUEXP coefficient estimate.[8] It thus seems safe to conclude that, although the EDUEXP coefficient estimate may very well reflect the effects of certain intangible neighborhood attributes to some degree, this component is probably not a very large one.

Given an average of 3.25 persons per household, a PARKEX coefficient of .00325 would imply that an increase in parks and recreation expenditure sufficient to raise per capita expenditure one dollar would be fully reflected in rental values. The coefficient estimate of .00228 falls somewhat short of this benchmark, implying that an expenditure increment of one dollar per household would increase rental values about seventy cents.

Given the nature of the fire protection variable (FIRE), an interpretation such as the foregoing is not possible. The coefficient estimate of .0528 does imply, however, that a substantial increase in fire department visibility, from 0.50 to 0.75 stations per square mile, for example, would increase annual rental values by about $13.[9] If this amount is compared with the typical annual fire insurance premium of about $100 for a dwelling unit in this sample, it can be seen that this is a fairly small figure.

It will be recalled that, in order to deal with the nonlinearity inherent in the relationship between the tax rate and rental value, the effective tax rate (TAXRT) was multiplied by a measure of size—the number of rooms (NROOMS)—to obtain the adjusted tax variable TRTNRMS. Since TRTNRMS has been constructed in this manner, the underlying coefficient of TAXRT can be obtained simply by multiplying the estimated coefficient of TRTNRMS by the number of rooms. In other words, since

$$\frac{\partial R}{\partial \text{TRTNRMS}} = \frac{1}{\text{NROOMS}} \cdot \frac{\partial R}{\partial \text{TAXRT}}$$

it follows that

$$\frac{\partial R}{\partial \text{TAXRT}} = \text{NROOMS} \cdot \frac{\partial R}{\partial \text{TRTNRMS}}$$

Since a typical dwelling unit in the sample has an annual rental value of $2,860, a TAXRT coefficient of .286 would imply that a change in the effective tax rate was completely reflected in rental value.[10] Since a typical dwelling unit has 6.15 rooms, a TRTNRMS coefficient of .0465 would imply that a change in the effective tax rate was completely reflected in rental value; that is, it was not capitalized. Correspondingly, a TRTNRMS coefficient of zero, and hence a TAXRT coefficient of zero, implies that a tax change will not be reflected in rental value; that is, it will be capitalized.

The TRTNRMS coefficient estimate is − .00336 for the single-family owner-occupied case. Although it takes an implausible negative sign, it is very small and is not significantly different from zero at the .05 level. Although this result thus provides some evidence for the proposition that tax rate changes are capitalized into property values in the sample communities, it should also be noted that the tax variable coefficient is measured imprecisely. In fact, neither the null hypothesis of complete capitalization of a tax change nor the null hypothesis that a tax change is completely reflected in rental values (that is, the null hypothesis that the TRTNRMS coefficient equals .0465) can be rejected at the .05 level.

To examine the effects of educational services on rental values further, it is useful to examine results of the market most likely to be relevant to households with children. The 114 dwelling units with four rooms or fewer were removed from the single-family owner-occupied sample under the assumption that they were predominantly outside the market of households containing school-age children. Column II of table 2–11 presents the results for this reduced sample of 1,991 dwelling units. Broadly, these results are quite similar to those reported in column I of the table. The null hypothesis that the coefficients of the three local public service variables are jointly equal to zero can again be rejected at the .005 level.[11] The coefficient of the education variable remains significant at the .01 level, while the coefficients of the fire variable is now significant at the .073 level. The null hypothesis that parks and recreational facilities do not influence rental values still cannot be rejected.

While the effects of education and parks and recreation on rental values change little, the coefficient of the fire protection variable increases from .0528 to .129. A substantial increase in fire department visibility from 0.50 to 0.75 stations per square mile now increases rental values by about $32.

To examine how the evaluation of local public services varies across submarkets, results are presented for white-collar and non-white-collar subsamples. The white-collar subsample consists of the single-family owner-occupied dwelling units located in the 43 census tracts classified in table 2–2 as having 60 percent or more of the males in white-collar occupations. The non-white-collar subsample consists of the dwelling units in the remaining 60 census tracts, which are classified in table 2–2 as either having 60 percent or more of the males in blue-collar occupations or being mixed (that is, being neither 60 percent white-collar nor 60 percent blue-collar).

Table 2–12 presents the results for the white-collar and the non-white-collar subsamples of 960 and 1,145 dwellings, respectively. In general, neighborhood amenities are valued more in white-collar neighborhoods than they are in the remaining neighborhoods. As with the total samples, no evidence of the importance of perceived safety is found. As discussed earlier, this may very well stem from the inadequacy of the crime variable.

The employment accessibility variable takes an unanticipated negative sign for the white-collar subsample. It may be that, for this subsample, industrial disamenities correlated with this measure play a more decisive role in housing expenditure choices than does job accessibility, while the reverse may be true for households in the non-white-collar subsample.

The local public service variables are more important determinants of rental values in the white-collar subsample than they are in the non-white-collar subsample. The hypothesis that the public services as a group do not matter can be rejected at the .005 level for the white-collar case,[12] but can be rejected only at the .10 level for the non-white-collar case.[13] The white-collar educational services coefficient estimate (.00455) is much larger than the non-white-collar coefficient (.00071), implying that a given increase in educational expenditure would be more than fully reflected in rental value in the white-collar case but that only about half of a given increase would be reflected in the non-white-collar case. In addition, while the white-collar coefficient is significantly different from zero at the .01 level, the non-white-collar coefficient is significant only at the .10 level. Although the non-white-collar educational services coefficient estimate falls short of the benchmark coefficient of .00150, it is not significantly different from it at the .05 level.

As discussed earlier, the estimated implicit price of a public service provides us with a single point on the demand curve for that service. Thus, the demand for education in the white-collar and non-white-collar submarkets cannot be quantitatively compared. It can, however, be inferred from our results that, for implict prices falling between those found for these two submarkets, the demand for education is higher in the white-collar submarket, since both the implicit price and the current supply are higher in the white-collar submarket. In other words, if the (fixed) white-collar education supply is represented by a vertical supply curve that is to the right of the corresponding non-white-collar one, then the higher white-collar implicit price necessarily implies a greater demand in the relevant price range.

None of the fire protection or parks and recreational coefficient estimates are significantly different from zero at the .05 level. However, the magnitude of the white-collar parks and recreation coefficient (.00943) is considerably greater than in the results for the total owner-occupied sample, implying that an expenditure increment of one dollar per household would increase rental values about $2.90. This coefficient, however, is not significantly greater than its counterpart in the total sample results.

Given that a typical dwelling unit in a white-collar neighborhood has a higher rental value ($3,430) and is larger (6.47 rooms) than its counterpart in the total sample, a TRTNRMS coefficient of .0530 would imply that a change in the effective property tax rate would be reflected fully in rental value. The estimated white-collar tax variable coefficient of .0337 implies

Table 2–12
Estimated Implicit Prices, Owner-Occupied Single-Family White-Collar Subsample and Owner-Occupied Single-Family Non-White-Collar Subsample

Variable	White-Collar Subsample (N = 960)	Non-White-Collar Subsample (N = 1,145)
Constant	−2.64	.376
	(.647)	(.570)
Structure		
NROOMS	.264	.518
	(.101)	(.0996)
LOTSIZ	1.72	2.08
	(.128)	(.109)
AGEDUM1 (25+ yrs.)	−.907	−.318
	(.110)	(.9765)
AGEDUM2 (15–24 yrs.)	−.979	−.161
	(.105)	(.0768)
AGEDUM3 (6–14 yrs.)	−.439	−.170
	(.0858)	(.0591)
Neighborhood		
MEDRMS	.257	−.0542
	(.0583)	(.0678)
DENSITY	−0763	−.0147
	(.0238)	(.00391)
GOLF	.316	−.0867
	(.0755)	(.0528)
MOUNTS	−.0335	.172
	(.0750)	(.0532)
CRIME	.0158	.00837
	(.0102)	(.00701)
Accessibility		
JOBACC	−.188	.192
	(.108)	(.0755)
Public services		
EDUEXP	.00455	.000710
	(.000784)	(.000537)
PARKEX	.00943	−.00198
	(.0101)	(.00667)
FIRE	−.0401	−.0926
	(.130)	(.122)
Tax variable		
TRTNRMS	.0337	−.163
	(.0472)	(.0497)
SSR	18.23	17.93
SE	.139	.126

Left-hand variable is imputed gross rental value, in thousands of dollars.
All observations are weighted by1/NROOMS.

that almost 65 percent of a given change in the effective property tax rate will be reflected in rental value. The coefficient estimate is imprecise, however; neither the null hypothesis that a tax change will not be reflected in rental value nor the null hypothesis that a tax change will be fully reflected in rental value can be rejected. In the non-white-collar case, the tax variable coefficient estimate takes an implausible negative sign.

Results for Rental Dwelling Units

Households that occupy rental units have fewer children on average. Does this mean that they will place less value on the quality of educational services because they currently use less of them? Or will good schools still be valued for other reasons, such as anticipation of a change in household size? These questions raise the related issues of sense of identification with a community and anticipated duration of stay. Also to be considered is the possibility that owner-occupants will desire higher levels of public services in order to increase the asset value of their dwellings. Because of such considerations, it is at least possible that potential owner-occupants may value public services more than potential renters do.

Given that the desired structure type is hardly invariant with respect to household type (especially presence, number, and age of children), separate results are estimated for different structure types. An alternative procedure would have been to estimate a single equation for all rental units in the sample, employing dummy variables to account for the structure-type differences. This procedure was not used, however, because of the danger of not adequately accounting for the differences between structure-type subsamples.

Two structure types were chosen for estimation: rental units in two-to-four-unit structures and rental units in five-to-nineteen-unit structures. Results for single-family rental units would have provided an interesting comparison with those for single-family owner-occupied units, but the very nature of the single-family rental market prevented obtaining good estimates. This market is the most difficult to analyze of those considered here. Many of the units are being rented by their owners only temporarily, and the contract rent frequently is influenced by such considerations as the short duration of the rental period and the fact that the dwelling is being rented for less than a market rent in exchange for the confidence that the premises and personal possessions will be well cared for during the owner's absence. Results for dwelling units in large structures (twenty or more units) also would have been useful for comparative purposes. The available data were inadequate, however.

Table 2–13 presents the means and standard deviations of the variables for the two rental samples. Compared to the single-family owner-occupied case (table 2–11), the average rental dwelling unit in either a two-to-four-unit structure or a five-to-nineteen-unit structure is smaller, with slightly fewer than four rooms, and has a considerably lower annual rental value. It is located in a community of somewhat smaller dwelling units than its counterpart, is better located with respect to employment opportunities, and is located in a community with higher levels of provision of all three public services.

Table 2–14 presents the results for the two rental subsamples: the two-to-four-unit structure subsample (217 dwelling units) and the five-to-nineteen-unit structure subsample (277 dwelling units). With the exception of the perceived safety variable, neighborhood amenities are valued less by renters than by owner-occupants. Unlike the case in the owner-occupant results, the perceived safety variable becomes a reasonably important determinant of rental values. For rental units in two-to-four-unit structures, the null hypothesis that the CRIME coefficient is equal to zero can be rejected at the .054 level of significance. For rental units in five-to-nineteen-unit structures, the CRIME coefficient is roughly the same size but somewhat less precisely measured.

For rental units in two-to-four unit structures, the employment accessibility variable has a negligible effect on rental values, while for rental units in five-to-nineteen-unit structures the coefficient estimate not only takes an unanticipated negative sign but is of substantial magnitude and is almost significant at the .10 level. As was the case in the owner-occupied white-collar subsample, it is possible that a factor such as industrial disamenity is being represented in these samples by the employment accessibility variable.

For both the two-to-four-unit and the five-to-nineteen-unit subsamples, the hypothesis that the coefficients of the three local public service variables are jointly equal to zero can be rejected at the .005 level.[14] Educational services are important determinants of rental values in both cases. In fact, both EDUEXP coefficient estimates (.00156) and .00131, respectively) are fairly close to the benchmark coefficient of .00150, indicating that an expenditure increment will be fully reflected in rental values. Educational services are valued less in the rental cases than in the owner-occupied case, however. Although neither fire protection services nor parks and recreational services appear to be important in the market for dwelling units in two-to-four-unit structures, there is some evidence that fire protection services do matter in the case of five-to-nineteen-unit structures. In this case, the FIRE coeffi-

Table 2-13
Rental Dwelling Units in Two-to-Four-Unit Structures and Five-to-Nineteen-Unit Structures: Means and Standard Deviations

Variable	2-4-Unit Structures		5-19-Unit Structures	
	Mean	*Standard Deviation*	*Mean*	*Standard Deviation*
RENT	1.304	0.368	1.407	0.384
NROOMS	3.84	0.87	3.64	0.85
AGEDUM1	0.203	0.403	0.0699	0.255
AGEDUM2	0.138	0.346	0.0478	0.213
AGEDUM3	0.272	0.446	0.3971	0.489
MEDRMS	4.60	0.62	4.49	0.69
DENSITY	7.02	6.70	6.64	6.52
GOLF	0.272	0.446	0.342	0.474
MOUNTS	0.184	0.389	0.202	0.402
CRIME	14.84	3.66	14.58	3.94
JOBACC	1.299	0.427	1.292	0.457
EDUEXP	572.6	51.5	586.9	54.7
FIRE	0.545	0.265	0.534	0.271
PARKEX	8.46	2.57	8.68	3.21
TRTNRMS	7.74	1.87	7.26	1.88

cient is significantly different from zero at the .075 level, and its magnitude of .113 implies that the hypothesized increase in fire department visibility from 0.50 to 0.75 stations per mile would increase annual rental values by about $28.

In both rental cases, the coefficient estimate of the tax variable takes an unanticipated negative sign and is sufficiently imprecisely measured so that no meaningful hypotheses can be rejected.

Concluding Comments

In chapter 1 and this chapter, the effects of levels of provision of three local public services on rental values have been examined for a number of sub-markets in the San Francisco Bay Area. Considerable evidence has been presented that is consistent with a weak version of the Tiebout hypothesis. At current levels of provision, households place a positive valuation on educational services; from this, it can be inferred that, at current levels of pro-

Table 2–14
Estimated Implicit Prices, Rental Dwelling Units in Two-to-Four-Unit Structures and Five-to-Nineteen-Unit Structures

Variable	2-4-Unit Structures (N = 217)	5-19-Unit Structures (N = 277)
Constant	−.0470	.629
	(.403)	(.367)
Structure		
NROOMS	.278	.314
	(.201)	(.191)
AGEDUM1 (25+ yrs.)	−.320	−.390
	(.0495)	(.0542)
AGEDUM2 (15–24 yrs.)	−.244	−.303
	(.0563)	(.0782)
AGEDUM3 (6–14 yrs.)	−.127	−.230
	(.0466)	(.0348)
Neighborhood		
MEDRMS	.0168	−.0150
	(.0314)	(.0138)
DENSITY	.00270	−.00609
	(.00304)	(.00403)
GOLF	.0258	−.00886
	(.0435)	(.0354)
MOUNTS	.0488	−.0288
	(.0565)	(.0646)
CRIME	−.00947	−.00950
	(.00589)	(.00701)
Accessibility		
JOBACC	−.00874	−.106
	(.0578)	(.0655)
Public services		
EDUEXP	.00156	.00131
	(.000591)	(.000552)
PARKEX	−.00843	−.0122
	(.00769)	(.00894)
FIRE	−.0304	.113
	(.0987)	(.0786)
Tax variable		
TRTNRMS	−.0446	−.0.773
	(.0989)	(.0974)
SSR	.9829	1.683
SE	.0708	.0809

Left-hand variable is rental value, in thousands of dollars.
All observations are weighted by 1/NROOMS.

vision, educational services indeed matter in the choice of residential location. Although plausible results were obtained for parks and recreational services in several cases, the estimates were quite imprecise. Evidence of the importance of fire protection services was found in two of the six cases considered, and the magnitude of the effect of fire protection on rental values was plausible.

The pattern of results across tenure categories—owners versus renters—and across the neighborhood types used to stratify the sample—white-collar versus non-white-collar—can be conveniently summarized. At current levels of provision, owners place a higher value on marginal changes in local education expenditures than do renters, while owners in white-collar neighborhoods value such changes more than do owners in non-white-collar neighborhoods. Expenditures on parks and recreation are valued more by households in larger residences and households in white-collar neighborhoods, at least among the owner subsamples. Fire protection services also seem to be valued more by households in larger residences.

Notes

1. U.S. Bureau of the Census, *Census of Housing, 1960* (1963).

2. Unfortunately, nominal property tax rates could only be adjusted by countywide assessment ratios. For empirical examinations of systematic biases in property tax assessments, see Case (1978), Meador and Pollakowski (1981), and Pollakowski (1977).

3. The R^2 is not presented in the results that follow. This is because the R^2 calculated by the regression package refers to the homoscedastic model rather than the original heteroscedastic model. In other words, the calculated R^2 refers to the ability of the model to explain IMPRTL/NROOMS, not IMPRTL. When the model was estimated in its original nonstandardized form for several of the cases considered in chapter 2, the values of R^2 obtained were as follows: total sample owner-occupied case: .53; two-to-four-unit structure rental case: .47; five-to-nineteen-unit structure rental case: .46. If a precise measure of the R^2 of the original model were required, it could be obtained by computing the simple correlation between IMPRTL and the predicted values of IMPRTL obtained by multiplying the matrix of observations on the original nonstandardized right-hand variables by the vector of estimated coefficients. It was believed, however, that the extra degree of precision thus obtained was unnecessary.

4. A possible explanation for the CRIME variable not having a negative effect on rental values is that it reflects both property and personal crimes, and it might be expected that higher rental values (and hence higher property values) attract more property crime than do lower rental values. CRIME is specified as an endogenous right-hand variable in the use of two-stage least squares, however, and this specification should produce a CRIME coefficient that basically does not reflect the influence of property values on the felony crime rate.

5. The F test is described in Fisher (1970).

6. The value of the appropriate F statistic (with 3 and 2,083 degrees of freedom) is 37.377, which is significant at the .005 level.

7. One-tailed tests of significance were employed, since there were *a priori* beliefs about the signs of the coefficients.

8. Two of the neighborhood (census tract) variables employed in earlier regression runs were the median number of years of school attended by males aged twenty-five years and over and the percentage of the male occupants in white-collar occupations.

9. The mean number of fire stations per square mile for the cities in this sample is about 0.50.

10. Consider the case in which the effective tax rate increases from 2.00 to 2.10. If this tax change is fully reflected in rental value, rental value (measured in thousands of dollars) changes from

$$R_G = (r + s + q + t)V$$
$$= (.05 + .015 + .015 + .0200)\,(28.6)$$
$$= \$2.860$$

to

$$R_G = (.05 + .015 + .015 + .0210)\,(28.6)$$
$$= \$2.8886$$

where the market value of the property, V, is also measured in thousands of dollars. Since R_G has increased by \$.0286 (measured in thousands of dollars), a TAXRT coefficient of .286 will imply that a given tax change will be fully reflected in rental value.

11. The value of the appropriate F statistic (with 3 and 1,969 degrees of freedom) is 16.647, which is significant at the .005 level.

12. The value of the appropriate F statistic (with 3 and 938 degrees of freedom) is 18.358, which is significant at the .005 level.

13. The value of the appropriate F statistic (with 3 and 1,123 degrees of freedom) is 2.087.

14. For the two-to-four-unit rental subsample, the value of the appropriate F statistic (with 3 and 196 degrees of freedom) is 5.523, which is significant at the .005 level. For the five-to-nineteen-unit rental subsample, the value of the appropriate F statistic (with 3 and 256 degrees of freedom) is 5.040, which is also significant at the .005 level.

**Part II
Neighborhood Amenities,
Energy Prices, and Urban
Housing Markets**

3

Economic Valuation of a Neighborhood Amenity: Water-Related Open Space

This chapter examines several issues concerning an important neighborhood amenity: water-related urban open space. A model of the determination of optimal water-related open space is presented, and hedonic price equations for housing are estimated to learn the value of open space and to determine the optimal amount.

Many American urban areas contain substantial amounts of shoreline property facing rivers, lakes, and oceans. In many of these areas, shoreline development and use is a growing public policy issue. Economists, however, have not yet turned their attention to the economic significance of the existence and width of the undeveloped apron offering public use and access to bodies of water in urban areas. There are several important issues to be considered here. May we expect the urban land market to provide a solution that is Pareto efficient? Have public agencies acted in a socially optimal way through zoning and other building restrictions? What contribution can studies of the determinants of property values make to our understanding of these issues? In this chapter, an examination of these issues is begun and empirical results are presented for a specific metropolitan area containing numerous bodies of water.[1]

In the next section, the discussion of the choice of a bundle of housing attributes is extended to include water-related open space and proximity to bodies of water as housing attributes. This is followed by a brief review of the process of formation of implicit attribute prices. Next, the data set, which consists of observations on individual Seattle dwelling units near bodies of water, both with and without open space, is presented and discussed. Results are then presented for estimating hedonic price equations in order to obtain estimated implicit prices of water-related open space and proximity to bodies of water. After a discussion of the value placed on these housing attributes by households, the determination of optimal water-related open space is discussed. A model of optimal open space is specified, and estimates of the optimal width of a band of water-related open space are presented for the Seattle sample.

This chapter is based on Gardner M. Brown, Jr., and Henry O. Pollakowski, "Economic Valuation of Shoreline," *The Review of Economics and Statistics* 59, no. 3 (August 1977): 272–278. Published for Harvard University. Copyright 1977 by North-Holland Publishing Company. Used with permission.

Water-Related Open Space and Property Values

As discussed in chapter 1, a given housing unit is usefully characterized as consisting of a bundle of attributes that describe the structure itself, the land on which it is built, and the relevant locational characteristics. Water-related open space, referred to here as setback, and proximity to water are thus viewed as two locational attributes of the housing bundle. At any given time there exists a given distribution over space of the supplies of these attributes. This assumption is made since the housing stock is altered only slowly over time and because some attributes, such as certain neighborhood amenities, are supplied perfectly inelastically.

On the demand side, assuming a given spatial distribution of employment and a given distribution of preferences and income over households, a distribution over space of demands for these attributes may be envisioned. The housing market is thus viewed as consisting of implicit markets for each of the attributes of housing, broadly defined, and it is assumed that, at any given time, a vector of implicit short-run equilibrium prices exists. Estimated implicit prices of the dwelling unit attributes can be obtained by estimating hedonic price equations in which dwelling unit selling price is regressed on the variables representing the attributes that constitute the housing package.[2]

The Sample

The sample areas or neighborhoods are located in Seattle, a city that is ideal for the purpose of this chapter because it contains numerous and varied bodies of water, some surrounded by open space and some not. Numerous potential sample areas located close to bodies of water were considered for use. The most important objective was to achieve a relatively high degree of homogeneity within and across areas. Neighborhoods chosen were similar in topography, non-water-related neighborhood characteristics, and accessibility. Areas that contained or were adjacent to large commercial zones were eliminated from consideration, and only areas that were adjacent to bodies of water used extensively for recreation purposes were employed. The number of feasible choices of areas with setback was severely limited by lack of variation in the width of the setback in numerous areas. Finally, a number of otherwise acceptable areas were eliminated because of physical obstructions, such as railroad tracks that inhibited ready access to the water's edge or setback.

This selection procedure yielded three areas: one exhibiting significant variation in setback width and two with no setback. Each of these areas is an almost exclusively single-family residential area, and, since each area is within the Seattle city limits, nominal property tax rates do not vary. One of the areas without setback is located on Lake Washington, a very large inland body of water. The remaining two areas encircle two smaller lakes, Green Lake (with setback) and Haller Lake (without setback). The boundaries of the sample areas were based, in part, on previous work by others, which indicated that the contribution of a water resource to property values generally is not significant beyond 4,000 feet from the water's edge.[3] In one area (Green Lake), 4,000 feet was used. In the other areas, 2,200 feet was selected because the criteria employed here for homogeneity would have been violated had a greater distance been included. In one area, for example, a change in topography at a distance of 3,000 feet was accompanied by a sharp change in racial composition of the dwellers.

The housing data employed consist of market sales data for dwelling units in these areas sold during the period 1969–1974. These housing data were obtained from real estate sources.[4] This data source includes, for each observation, selling price and a good description of the structural attributes. The selling price data were deflated to constant 1967 dollars by use of a local price index for single-family residential sales within the Seattle metropolitan area.[5] The open space variable employed was constructed by measuring the width of setback area abutting the water and closest to the dwelling unit in question. The distance to waterfront was measured as the shortest linear distance from the dwelling unit to the nearby waterfront.

Empirical Results

The regression results are presented in tables 3–1 and 3–2. The results presented employ a linear functional form, with setback size and distance to waterfront appearing in log form. Limited experimentation with functional forms other than the linear one did not substantively alter the basic results.[6] The natural logarithm of setback size is employed, reflecting the assumption that, as setback width was increased, the marginal contribution to housing value would decrease. Similarly, it is assumed that, as distance to the waterfront increases, property values decrease at a decreasing rate. Thus, distance to waterfront also appears in natural logarithmic form. Since tests on preliminary regression runs indicated the presence of heteroscedasticity, all observations are weighted by 1/living area.

Table 3-1 presents the results for Green Lake, the setback area. As mentioned earlier, the width of the setback varies a good deal as one moves around the lake, making this an especially appropriate area to study. Table 3-2 presents results for a pooled sample consisting of the two areas without setback. In both cases, nearly all the coefficient estimates are of the hypothesized signs, and the explanatory power of the right-hand variables is quite high.

Table 3-1
Results for Green Lake Area

Variable	Coefficient	Standard Error
Constant	15700	3400
Living area (sq. ft.)	3.38	1.17
Age of house	−73.3	15.4
Average room size	−5.51	7.25
Number of fireplaces	1120	415
Number of car garage	674	455
Number of rooms first story	−311	265
Number of bathrooms	2830	607
D = 1 if basement	1260	464
D = 1 if dishwasher	2010	784
D = 1 if good or excellent quality	289	486
D = 1 if range and oven	255	748
D = 1 if hot-water heating	1040	1140
D = 1 if wall or floor furnace heating	−2200	801
D = 1 if electric heating	−1660	903
Lot size (sq. ft.)	−9.247	0.195
D = 1 if view	573	693
Log of distance to waterfront	−1770	762
Log of individual setback size	1230	744
SSR = 197		
SE = 1.66		
R^2 = .84		

Sources: Selling price and structural characteristics: SREA Market Data Center, Inc., *Single Family Residential Sales* (Seattle, April 1969 to June 1974). Distance to waterfront and setback size: measured on local maps.

Left-hand variables is selling price (deflated to 1967 dollars).

All observations are weighted by 1/living area. $N = 90$.

The results bearing on the value of distance to waterfront and size of open space are quite interesting. Applying the appropriate one-tailed t tests, the null hypothesis that the coefficient estimate of the distance to waterfront variable is zero can be rejected at the .01 level in each case. In the setback case (table 3-1), the null hypothesis that the setback coefficient estimate is zero can be rejected at the .051 level.

The effect of variation in setback in the Green Lake area is substantial. A dwelling unit located in an area close to a 200-foot-wide setback will sell for about $850 more than a comparable one located near a 100-foot-wide setback area. This same dwelling unit, if located near a 300-foot-wide setback area, would sell for about $1,350 more than if it were located near a 100-foot-wide setback area.

The estimates of premiums paid for proximity to shoreline are very plausible ones for the Seattle area, and, as expected, this premium declines

Table 3–2
Results for Areas without Setback

Variable	Coefficient	Standard Error
Constant	16500	3580
Living area (sq. ft.)	4.17	1.84
Age of house	−74.6	40.0
Average room size	−13.8	11.6
Number of fireplaces	417	608
Number of car garage	1510	617
Number of rooms first story	−44.4	399
Number of bathrooms	5120	1190
D = 1 if basement	300	831
D = 1 if dishwasher	308	888
D = 1 if good or excellent quality	289	649
D = 1 if range and oven	298	839
D = 1 if hot-water heating	5790	3380
D = 1 if wall or floor furnace heating	−540	998
D = 1 if electric heating	−2250	1110
Lot size (sq. ft.)	0.235	0.104
D = 1 if view	1340	1110
D = 1 if in Haller Lake area	−1730	706
Log of distance to waterfront	−2790	548
SSR = 380		
SE = 2.33		
R^2 = .78		

Left-hand variable is selling price (deflated to 1967 dollars). All observations are weighted by 1/living area. $N = 89$.

with distance to waterfront much more rapidly in the case of no setback than in the setback case. Applying the appropriate F test, the null hypothesis that the respective coefficient estimates of the distance to waterfront variable are equal can be rejected at the .05 level. In the case of no setback, three-fourths of the location value of proximity to water has been lost at a distance of 300 feet from the waterfront.

Determination of Optimal Open Space

The next question to be examined is whether the amount of open space around the water bodies studied is optimal. A necessary first step is to decide how the estimated hedonic price equation can be used to answer this question.

First, consider the measurement of benefits of open space. Given that willingness to pay is the appropriate measure of the value of open space, we wish to obtain an estimate of the area under the demand function for open space. The estimated hedonic price function itself is most appropriately viewed as an opportunity locus facing households in the housing market.[7] Taking the derivative of this function with respect to setback gives a marginal implicit price function. This function, which will be downward-sloping and convex from below in the case of setback, is most appropriately viewed as the locus of the marginal willingness-to-pay functions of households.

Assume that the characteristics embedded in housing are not obtainable by the purchase of other products and that utility functions are weakly separable between housing service characteristics and other characteristics. If we then assume that migration among metropolitan areas is possible, that households have equal incomes, and that households have identical utility functions, it follows that all households will have identical marginal willingness-to-pay functions.[8] In this case, the estimated marginal implicit price function may be appropriately viewed as the marginal willingness-to-pay function, and an estimate of the value of open space may be obtained from the function we have estimated. Given the nature of the assumptions necessary to make this calculation, there is good reason to regard the results obtained as indicating only rough orders of magnitude.[9,10]

The determination of optimal open space is straightforward. If those who benefit from the water-related open space are also the owners or renters of property, then the added value for all property affected by slightly changing the amount of open space should just offset the cost of buying the property or the added space. Since a land value gradient can be computed from the estimated hedonic price equation, enough information is available to perform a rough calculation.[11]

On the assumption that the boundary of a water body is well described by a circle with radius r, and that all properties have the same area A, the number of properties within a band of land of width Q from the water's edge is given by

$$N(Q) = (\Pi/\bar{A})(2rQ + Q^2).$$

The marginal number of properties at Q is

$$N'(Q) = (2\Pi/\bar{A})(r + Q).$$

Optimal open space is found by maximizing with respect to open space, Q_s.

$$W = \int_{Q_s}^{\bar{Q}} N'(Q)V(Q,Q_s)dQ$$

$$- \int_0^{\bar{Q}_s} N'(Q)V(Q,Q_s)dQ. \tag{3.1}$$

where $V(Q, Q_s)$ is the value of a property whose distance to the water is Q, Q_s is the width of the strip of open space around the water, and $\bar{Q}$ is the distance from the shoreline beyond which it is assumed that properties no longer benefit from this open space.

The first expression on the right-hand side of equation 3.1 represents the benefits of setback or open space, embodying the assumption that all property located between the edge of the open space and $\bar{Q}$ benefits from open space. The second expression on the right-hand side of the equation represents the opportunity cost of open space—the foregone private value of each property that could have been located between the water's edge and the terminus of the open space.

Figure 3-1 illustrates the nature of the problem. In the absence of any setback or public access, the value of all property at the lakeshore rim equals $N_0 V_0$. The value of property declines with distance until a distance of $\bar{Q}$ is reached. When setback equals Q_s, the value of all property at that distance from water is higher than it would have been in the absence of setback. The optimal setback occurs when the loss of private property value near the shore, $Q_0 N_0 V_0 A Q_s$, is compensated by the gain to remaining properties, $ABCE$, from additional setback.

The necessary condition for a maximum is

$$\int_{Q_s}^{\bar{Q}} N'(Q) h(Q_s) dQ - \int_0^{Q_s} N'(Q) h(Q_s) dQ$$

$$- 2N'(Q_s) V(Q_s, Q_s) = 0$$

where $h(Q_s)$ denotes the inverse demand function for open space and is equal to $\partial V(Q, Q_s) / \partial Q_s$. After noting that $h(Q_s)$ is independent of Q, revising yields

$$h(Q_s) \left[\int_{Q_s}^{\bar{Q}} N'(Q) dQ - \int_{Q_0}^{Q_s} N'(Q) dQ \right]$$

$$= 2N'(Q_s) V(Q_s, Q_s).$$

A comparison between actual and optimal open space is made by drawing on the results for Green Lake and by assuming that the area under the marginal implicit price function accurately reflects willingness to pay. Optimal open space is about 100 feet, compared to the actual average distance of about 300 feet. At 100 feet, the net benefit of open space is about $13 million, falling about $.5 million when the amount of setback is 200 feet on average. Computed net benefits fall by somewhat more than $1 million (about 10 percent) when the radius of open space is increased to present levels.

Of course, many people in the greater Seattle area benefit from the use

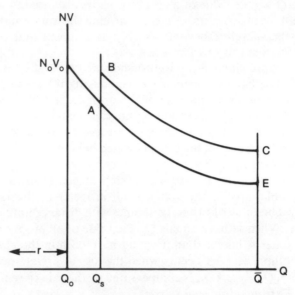

Figure 3–1. Open Space, Distance to Waterfront, and Property Value

of the open space around Green Lake but do not live within the 4,000-foot perimeter specified in the sample. The estimate made here is a lower bound to the measurement of total and marginal benefits of open space, and this must be borne in mind in interpreting the calculations. It cannot be concluded confidently that optimal open space is lower than actual. Note, also, that the net benefit function is fairly flat. Underestimated marginal benefits amounting to less than a capitalized value of $100 per house would shift the optimal width of open space to 200 feet.[12]

Open Space: A Public Decision

It is appropriate to consider open space as a public good so long as partial rivalry in consumption (congestion) is not an important consideration. Although an existing owner of property can capture, through exchange, a portion of the value of open space should it appreciate—this being the motivating assumption of our empirical investigation—owners of property cannot individually determine the optimum open space. Some form of collective action is called for. Alternatively, the right to determine the open space could be granted, with or without compensation, to an omniscient entrepreneur, admonishing him to behave in a manner compatible with a competitive solution. But there is a more unconventional aspect to the problem studied, which makes the regulated private solution a cumbersome one.

Our empirical results indicate that the value of a property falls with distance from the water.[13] Therefore, the marginal cost of property exchanged in a competitive market is falling as we move away from the water. Since the average cost is greater than marginal cost, an entrepreneur who seeks an optimal amount of open space cannot cover his costs if he follows the competitive prescription of setting price equal to marginal cost of open space for all beneficiaries. Either the entrepreneur must be permitted to deviate from marginal cost pricing or he must receive a subsidy. The other major solution is for the public sector to take direct responsibility for providing optimal open space. Falling cost plus inability to exclude are two traditional economic reasons that the determination of open space around water bodies is likely to remain very much a public issue and will be resolved by the public sector.

With falling marginal costs of acquiring open space, of course, a final calculation must be made to insure that the total benefits of open space are greater than the total costs. This condition holds for our representative area.[14]

Notes

1. More generally, this chapter extends recent economic work that has produced quantitative measures of value for phenomena previously restricted to qualitative expression. This work includes related research that derives the implicit value of natural environmental attributes or activities that use natural environment intensively, including the work by Hammack and Brown (1974) on waterfowl; Castle, Singh, and Brown (1964) and Mathews and Brown (1970) on sports salmon fishing; and Davis (1964) and Krutilla and Fisher (1975) on wilderness. Krutilla and Fisher both refers to and summarizes interesting related research by C.J. Cicchetti and V.K. Smith.

2. Hedonic price equations employing microdata and specifying the bundle of housing services in an interesting manner include Kain and Quigley (1970), King (1973, 1975), and Grether and Mieszkowski (1974). The natural environmental attribute previously studied in this manner has been ambient air quality. See Freeman (1974), Polinsky and Shavell (1975, 1976), and Small (1975) for discussion of the theoretical issues involved in interpreting the results of the air quality studies and for further references.

3. See, for example, Dornbusch and Barrager (1972).

4. Sales data were obtained from the SREA Market Data Center, Inc., *Single Family Residential Sales* (Seattle, April 1969 to June 1974).

5. The price index for single-family residential sales was obtained from the Seattle Real Estate Research Committee, *Real Estate Research Report for the City of Seattle and Metropolitan Area* (Seattle, Fall 1974).

6. See Grether and Mieszkowski (1974) for a comparison of results of linear and semilogarithmic functional forms. Appendix A presents a general framework for choice of functional form for hedonic price equations.

7. See Freeman (1974) and Rosen (1974) for more detailed discussions of these matters.

8. Polinsky and Shavell (1976), assuming identical Cobb-Douglas utility functions and equal incomes, identify the demand function for air quality in a general equilibrium model.

9. If we wished to consider only very small changes in open space, it would not be necessary to assume identical preferences. Although separability between open space and all other characteristics must be assumed in this case, it may not be unduly restrictive, given the degree of change envisioned. See Small (1975) on this matter. We must further assume a zero income elasticity of demand for setback in order to make the estimated demand curve correspond to a compensated demand curve. The latter provides a conceptually preferable basis for estimating willingness to pay.

10. When the assumptions stated in the text cannot be made, Freeman (1974) proposes a pragmatic solution for estimating the value of environmental change. Simply compute the marginal benefit for each individual, using the hedonic price equation, find the mean value, and assume that the demand curve is linear. This demand curve will cut through the marginal hedonic price equation, revealing that people on the lower end of the ad hoc demand curve are willing to pay less than actually has been observed. This limitation is pointed out here without prejudging the practicality of the suggestion.

11. There may be added cost of restoring the purchased land to open-space quality if it was formerly developed, but this is an analytically inessential point.

12. The number of houses benefiting is about 6,300. The discussion is in terms of 100-foot increments to conform with customary lot dimensions.

13. This result also makes analytical sense in the setback case if the open space yields an unambiguous flow of favorable services. But it might not. Open space can attract groups of people who are noisy, thus creating a disamenity.

14. See Freeman (1979) and Brown and Pollakowski (1979) for further discussion of the theoretical basis for the public provision of water-related open space.

4

Measurement of the Effects of Space-Heating Fuel Prices on House Prices

The abrupt shifts in energy prices that have occurred since the 1973 oil embargo presumably have had major impacts on the markets for other goods. There has been very little theoretical or empirical research, however, on the magnitude of these impacts. In this chapter, hedonic price equations for housing are employed to measure the effect on house prices of changes in the prices of space-heating fuels.

A simple theoretical model is used to examine the relationship between fuel prices and house prices. It is shown that the magnitude of the effect on house prices of a given change in fuel prices is a function of the elasticity of demand for heating fuel, the expenditure on heating fuel, and the effect of changes in current fuel prices on expectations of future fuel prices. Thus, the magnitude of the effect on house prices of the changes in fuel prices that have occurred since the 1973 oil embargo is not obvious *a priori*. Empirical estimates of these effects are obtained using hedonic price equations. The results indicate that fuel price changes have resulted in significant changes in house prices, with lags of variable length between the changes in fuel prices and the corresponding changes in house prices.

Fuel Prices and House Prices

As was the case in earlier chapters, it is useful to conceive of housing as composed of a bundle of attributes, including both structural characteristics and locational amenities. The relationship between equilibrium house prices and the attributes can be represented as

$$H_j = f(Z_{ij}) \tag{4.1}$$

where H_j is the price of house j and Z_{ij} are the housing attributes.

One attribute that might affect the price of a house is the type of fuel used by the space-heating system. The effect of this attribute on house price will be a function of the relative price of the type of fuel used. To illustrate, consider a sample of houses that are heated by either fuel oil, f, or natural gas, g. For ease of exposition, it will be assumed that the demand curve for

This chapter is based on Robert Halvorsen and Henry O. Pollakowski, "The Effects of Fuel Prices on House Prices," *Urban Studies* 18 (June 1981):205–211. Copyright © 1981 by Urban Studies. Used with permission.

space-heating fuel is identical for occupants of otherwise identical oil-heated and gas-heated houses.[1] Given this assumption, if the price of fuel oil were equal to the price of natural gas, $P_f = P_g$, consumers would be indifferent in choosing between otherwise identical oil-heated and gas-heated houses, and the space-heat attribute would have no effect on house prices.[2] However, if the prices of fuel oil and natural gas were not equal, the space-heat attribute could affect house prices.

The magnitude of the effect of fuel prices on house prices is constrained by the possibility of changing the space-heat attribute by converting the heating system to use the lower-priced fuel. However, if conversion is prevented by a moratorium on acceptance of new customers for the cheaper fuel, or if it involves substantial capital costs, the effect of the space-heat attribute on house prices can be substantial.

The magnitude of the effect of fuel prices on house prices depends on the losses incurred as a result of the use of the higher-priced fuel. The nature of these losses is illustrated for the case $P_f > P_g$ in figure 4-1. The loss, in terms of consumer surplus, that a household would incur in period t as a result of using fuel oil rather than natural gas is equal to the area

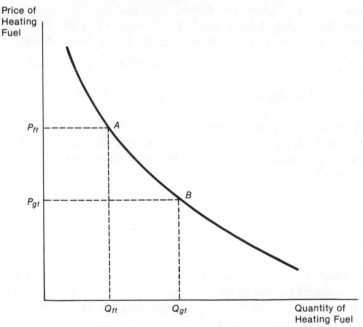

Source: Halvorsen and Pollakowski, "The Effects of Fuel Prices on House Prices," p. 206.

Figure 4-1. Demand for Heating Fuel

$P_{ft}ABP_{gt}$ in figure 4-1, where P_{ft} is the price of fuel oil in period t and P_{gt} is the price of natural gas. The magnitude of the loss, L_t, can be approximated by the formula

$$L_t = \frac{1}{2}(P_{ft} - P_{gt})(Q_{gt} + Q_{ft}) \tag{4.2}$$

where Q_{ft} is the amount of heating fuel that would be consumed at P_{ft}, and Q_{gt} is the amount of heating fuel that would be consumed at P_{gt}.[3]
Equation 3.2 can be rewritten as

$$L_t = \Delta P_t(Q_{gt} + \frac{1}{2}\Delta Q_t) \tag{4.3}$$

where $\Delta P_t = P_{ft} - P_{gt}$, and $\Delta Q_t = Q_{ft} - Q_{gt}$. By multiplying the second term in the parentheses by

$$\frac{P_{gt}}{P_{gt}} \frac{\Delta P_t}{\Delta P_t} \frac{Q_{gt}}{Q_{gt}}$$

and rearranging terms, we have

$$L_t = \Delta P_t\left[Q_{gt} + \frac{1}{2}\left(\frac{\Delta Q_t}{\Delta P_t} \frac{P_{gt}}{Q_{gt}}\Delta P_t \frac{Q_{gt}}{P_{gt}}\right)\right] \tag{4.4}$$

Noting that the term

$$\frac{\Delta Q_t}{\Delta P_t} \frac{P_{gt}}{Q_{gt}}$$

can be interpreted as the elasticity of demand for heating fuel, and multiplying by P_{gt}/P_{gt}, equation 3.4 can be written

$$L_t = \frac{\Delta P_t}{P_{gt}}\left[1 + \frac{1}{2}\left(E \frac{\Delta P_t}{P_{gt}}\right)\right]P_{gt}Q_{gt} \tag{4.5}$$

where E is the elasticity of demand for heating fuel. Thus, the loss to a household in period t from using fuel oil rather than natural gas will vary directly with the percentage difference in P_{ft} and P_{gt} and with total expenditures on heating fuel, and will vary inversely with the absolute value of the elasticity of demand for heating fuel.

The difference in the prices of otherwise identical houses using fuel oil and natural gas will reflect the capitalized value of all future anticipated losses. If the capitalized value of the anticipated losses from using fuel oil were less than the cost of converting the heating system to use natural gas, the effect of the space-heat attribute on house prices would be equal to

$$\sum_{t=0}^{T} \frac{L_t}{(1 + r)^t}$$

where T is the last period of the house's economic life, and r is the rate of discount. If the capitalized value of anticipated losses were greater than the cost of conversion, K, and conversion could be performed immediately, the effect of the space-heat attribute on house prices would be equal to the capital cost of conversion. Finally, if conversion could be performed only after a lag of τ periods, the effect of the space-heat attribute would be equal to

$$\frac{K}{(1 + r)^\tau} + \sum_{t=0}^{\tau} \frac{L_t}{(1 + r)^t} \qquad (4.6)$$

where the first term is the present value of the cost of conversion, and the second term is the present value of the losses incurred while awaiting conversion.

It is important to note that the magnitude of anticipated losses depends on expectations of future fuel prices. As a result, the effect on house prices of a change in relative fuel prices in a given period depends critically on the relationship between current prices and expectations of future prices. For example, suppose that the prices of fuels had been equal until period m, at which time the price of fuel oil increased relative to the price of natural gas. If the elasticity of expectations were unitary, the effect on house prices could be predicted in period m by calculating L_t for all future periods, using the value of P_f and P_g in period m. If, however, the change in fuel prices were expected to be transitory (that is, the elasticity of expectations were equal to zero), even a large change in fuel prices would have only a minor effect on house prices. Conversely, if a change in the relative prices of fuels were interpreted as reflecting a trend of increasing differences in fuel prices, the effect on house prices would be greater than in the case of a unitary elasticity of expectations.

In summary, the effect of changes in fuel prices on the prices of houses using different types of heating fuels will depend on the capitalized value of anticipated future losses of consumer surplus. The magnitude of the loss in a given period will depend on the degree to which the prices of fuels differ, the expenditures on heating fuel, and the elasticity of demand for heating fuel. The magnitude of anticipated future losses will depend on expected future prices and thus on the effect of current fuel prices on expected fuel prices. When conversion of the heating system is possible, an upper bound is imposed on the effect of the space-heat attribute on house prices equal to the present value of the costs of conversion and losses incurred while awaiting conversion.

Estimation Procedures

Substituting for L_t in expression 4.6 from equation 4.5, the effect of fuel prices on house prices is equal to

$$\frac{K}{(1 + r)^\tau} + \sum_{t=0}^{\tau} \frac{(\Delta P_t / P_{gt})[1 + (E/2)(\Delta P_t / P_{gt})] P_{gt} Q_{gt}}{(1 + r)^t} \tag{4.7}$$

If data were available on all the variables appearing in expression 4.7, the effect of fuel prices on house prices could be calculated directly. This is not the case, however. The most serious problem is that the fuel price variable in expression 4.7 refers to expected future prices, which are not observable. Although specification of a process for formation of price expectations from historical price data would permit the calculation of expected prices for use in expression 4.7, the results would be highly sensitive to the choice of this specification. Since little is known about the expectations formation process, little confidence could be placed in results based on assumptions about this process. The calculated values of the effects of fuel prices on house prices would also be sensitive to the estimates used for individual discount rates and for the elasticity of demand for heating fuel, both of which are uncertain.

An alternative procedure, which is employed here, is to use data on the actual sales price of oil-heated and gas-heated houses to estimate the effect of the space-heat attribute on house prices. The rationale for this procedure is that changes in the effect of the space-heat attribute over time reflect the effects of changes in fuel prices on house prices. This procedure provides a direct estimate of the value of expression 4.7.

The following basic hedonic price equation is employed to estimate the effects of fuel prices:

$$H_{jt} = f(Z_j, t, tZ_j) \tag{4.8}$$

where H_{jt} is the price in period t of house j, Z_j is a vector of housing characteristics, including type of space-heating fuel, t is time, and tZ_j is a set of interactions between time and type of fuel. This specification allows the estimation of the effects of fuel prices on house prices subject to minimal *a priori* restrictions. In particular, no restrictions are imposed with respect to the time path of the response of house prices to changes in fuel prices.

Since a hedonic price equation is a reduced-form equation reflecting both supply and demand influences, the appropriate functional form for the equation cannot be specified *a priori*. The functional forms most frequently used for hedonic house price equations are the linear and semi-log forms.[4] Both of these functional forms were estimated, and their performance was compared using the goodness-of-fit test suggested by Box and Cox (1964). The fit of the semi-log form was superior to that of the linear form.[5] The semi-log and linear forms were also compared by testing for homoscedasticity, using the F test proposed by Goldfeld and Quandt (1965). Homoscedasticity was accepted for the semi-log equation but rejected for the linear equation.[6] Because of its consistently superior performance, the results reported here are for the semi-log functional form.

The full specification of the semi-log equation is shown in table 4-1. The right-hand variables representing the characteristics embodied in the housing unit appear in either continuous or dummy variable form, with fuel type represented by a one/zero (fuel oil/natural gas) dummy. The sample was limited to houses using either fuel oil or natural gas for space heating.[7] As discussed later, interaction dummies are included in the equation to measure postembargo changes in the respective prices of oil-heated and gas-heated houses. The fuel-type dummy thus measures the effect on house prices of heating fuel type during the preembargo period. As shown in figure 4-2, the price of fuel oil relative to the price of natural gas was very stable during the preembargo period.

Year of sale is represented by a series of time dummies. Since preliminary results indicated that there were significant intrayear time effects in 1975, separate dummies are included for the first six months and second six months of 1975.

To obtain estimates of the effects of postembargo changes in fuel-oil and natural-gas prices on the prices of oil-heated and gas-heated houses, three interaction time and fuel-type dummy variables are included in the equation. The first interaction dummy is equal to one if the house was sold in 1974 and had oil heat and zero otherwise. The other two dummy variables indicate oil-heated houses sold in the first six months of 1975 and oil-heated houses sold in the second six months of 1975.

The noninteraction oil-heat dummy captures the effect of fuel type on house price in the preembargo period of stable relative energy prices. The housing characteristics variables capture the effects of changes in the average quality of houses sold, and the time dummies capture the effects of changes in the overall level of housing prices. Therefore, the coefficients of the interaction dummies provide the desired measures of the *ceteris paribus* effects on house prices of postembargo changes in relative fuel prices.

Table 4–1
Parameter Estimates

Variable	Coefficient	Standard Error
Constant	957.	6.25
Living area (sq. ft.)	.0289	.00321
Age of house	− .430	.0680
Lot size (sq. ft.)	.000296	.000617
Average room size	− .0814	.0233
Number of bathrooms	5.73	2.22
Number of fireplaces	4.97	1.52
Number of car garage	4.55	1.53
D = 1 if range and oven	4.26	2.63
D = 1 if dishwasher	5.93	2.79
D = 1 if remodeled	3.05	1.79
D = 1 if full basement	3.67	2.83
D = 1 if partial basement	2.77	3.07
D = 1 if view	5.55	4.28
D = 1 if oil-heated	− .00235	1.65
D = 1 if sold in 1971	1.66	2.10
D = 1 if sold in 1972	2.16	2.42
D = 1 if sold in 1973	11.4	2.45
D = 1 if sold in 1974	18.6	4.51
D = 1 if sold 1/75–6/75	40.8	5.71
D = 1 if sold 7/75–12/75	39.9	11.9
D = 1 if sold in 1974 and oil-heated	− 3.55	5.36
D = 1 if sold 1/75–6/75 and oil-heated	− 18.5	7.62
D = 1 if sold 7/75–12/75 and oil-heated	− .864	13.5

Number of observations = 269

SSR = 3.29

SE = .116

R^2 = .745

The parameter estimates and standard errors are multiplied by 100 for presentation here.
Left-hand variable is natural logarithm of selling price.

Data and Estimation Results

The sample area consists of a compact and well-defined Seattle neighborhood, commonly known as the Greenwood area.[8] This neighborhood is located about five miles from the Seattle central business district and consists primarily of single-family dwelling units. The neighborhood is an established one, mostly built up by the beginning of our sample period, which facilitates our aim of examining effects of changing fuel prices on the prices of existing houses.

The data employed consist of market sales data for single-family dwellings in this neighborhood sold during the period 1970–1975. The data were obtained from the same source of listings of real estate sales data employed in chapter 3.[9] For each observation, this data source includes selling price, date of sale, and a description of the characteristics constituting the dwelling, including the type of fuel used in the space-heating system.

Estimation results are shown in table 4-1. The performance of the hedonic model is quite good. The coefficient estimates take the anticipated signs wherever prior signs can reasonably be hypothesized, the magnitudes of the coefficients are usually plausible, and the estimates are generally reasonably precise.

The estimated coefficients of the interaction dummies measure the effects on house prices of postembargo changes in fuel prices. The price of fuel oil in Seattle began rising at the end of 1973, reached a level approximately twice the preembargo level by the end of 1974, and continued rising in 1975. The price of fuel oil relative to the price of natural gas began falling at the end of 1974, however, as the result of sharp increases in natural-gas prices. The time path of fuel-oil relative to natural-gas price is shown in figure 4-2.

The path of expected relative prices cannot be observed. Theories of the formation of price expectations generally imply, however, that the path of expected prices varies directly with the path of actual prices, though perhaps with significant lags in the adjustment of consumer expectations. Therefore, it would be expected that the price of oil-heated houses would first decline in response to the initial increase in the relative price of fuel oil and then at least partially recover in response to the later decline in the relative price of fuel oil.

The estimated coefficients of the interaction dummies indicate that this pattern of changes in house prices did in fact occur, with substantial lags between changes in energy prices and the corresponding changes in house prices. The estimate of the coefficient of the 1974 oil-heat interaction dummy is negative but fairly small, implying a *ceteris paribus* decrease of 3.5 percent in the price of oil-heated houses. The coefficient estimate for the interaction dummy for the first six months of 1975 is − 18.5. The implied effect on the price of oil-heated houses is a decrease of 16.9 percent.[10]

The estimated coefficient of the oil-heat interaction dummy for the second half of 1975 is negative but of negligible size. Thus, the results indicate that the negative impact on the prices of oil-heated houses of the postembargo increase in the price of fuel oil was almost completely eliminated by the subsequent increase in the price of natural gas.

The lag involved in the response of housing prices to the increase in the price of natural gas appears to have been considerably shorter than the lag in the earlier response to the increase in the price of fuel oil. A possible explanation is that the increasing perception of an energy crisis in the months

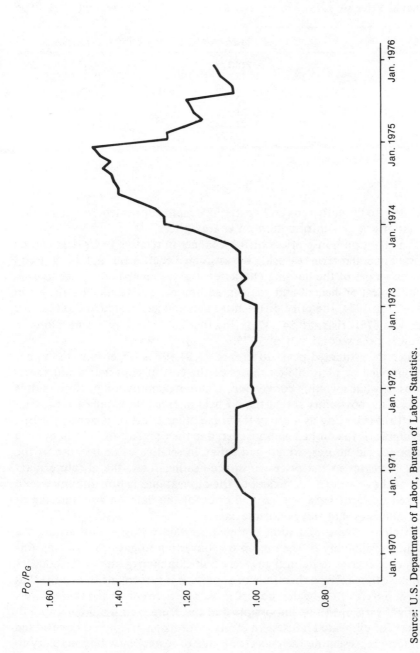

Source: U.S. Department of Labor, Bureau of Labor Statistics.

Note: January 1970 = 1.00.

Figure 4-2. Index of Fuel-Oil Price Relative to Natural-Gas Price in Seattle, January 1970–December 1975

Table 4-2
Estimated Price of a Typical House, by Year Sold and Heating-Fuel Type

Year Sold	Gas-Heated	Oil-Heated
1970	$18,128	$18,127
1971	18,431	18,431
1972	18,524	18,523
1973	20,325	20,324
1974	21,831	21,070
1/75–6/75	27,263	22,666
7/75–12/75	27,027	26,794

Source: Computed from results in table 4-1.

subsequent to the embargo resulted in more rapid adjustment of consumers' expectations to new information on energy prices.

The effect on house prices of the changes in relative fuel prices can be expressed in dollar terms by using the estimated coefficients in table 4-1 and the mean values of the housing characteristics to calculate the price in each year of typical oil-heated and gas-heated houses. The results are shown in table 4-2. In 1974, the price differential between gas-heated and oil-heated houses was $761, rising to $4,597 during the first half of 1975 and falling to $233 during the second half of 1975.

Since the estimated peak difference of $4,597 is larger than the upper bound implied by plausible estimates of the cost of conversion and short-term losses while awaiting conversion, a closer examination of this result is in order. One possibility is that the oil-heat interaction dummy for the first half of 1975 is serving as a proxy for some other effect of the energy crisis. For example, if the oil-heated houses sold in the first half of 1975 happened to be large, old houses, which had fallen in relative value because of the general increases in the prices of space-heating fuels, the absolute magnitude of the estimated coefficient of the oil-heat interaction dummy would be biased upward. However, examination of the data on size and age of houses indicates that this is not the case.

An alternative explanation is that uncertainty existed concerning the continued availability of the option of converting to gas heat. During this period, conversions to natural gas were halted in many parts of the country in response to perceived shortfalls of supply. It is reasonable to assume that potential buyers of oil-heated houses in Seattle were concerned that conversion might turn out to be impossible and therefore would bid correspondingly less for oil-heated houses. In effect, expression 4.7 should have added to it a term representing the expected value of losses caused by inability to convert to natural gas. This term would equal the perceived probability of a conversion moratorium times the loss in the event of such a moratorium.

Concluding Comments

In this chapter, procedures are developed for examining the *ceteris paribus* effects of the changes in relative fuel prices on house prices. A hedonic price equation is estimated, which includes variables representing fuel type, time, and interactions between time and fuel type. The results indicate that post-embargo changes in fuel prices did have significant effects on house prices, but with substantial lags between changes in fuel prices and the corresponding changes in house prices. The largest measured effect in dollar terms is a decrease of $4,597 in the price of a typical oil-heated house in the first half of 1975.

Notes

1. If fuel oil and natural gas are perceived to differ with respect to such characteristics as cleanliness and convenience, the demand curves will not be identical unless the prices of the fuels are adjusted for quality. The assumption of identical demand curves simplifies the exposition without affecting the qualitative characteristics of the conclusions.

2. As discussed later, the empirical results indicate that the space-heat attribute had no effect on the prices of oil-heated and gas-heated houses in Seattle in the years immediately preceding 1973.

3. The approximation will be exact if the demand curve is linear.

4. See chapters 1, 2, and 3 and King (1973) for examples employing a linear functional form. See Grether and Mieszkowski (1974) and Kain and Quigley (1970) for examples employing both linear and semi-log functional forms. For a general treatment of the choice of functional form for hedonic price equations, see appendix A.

5. The chi-squared test statistic for equivalence of the specifications is 57.9, compared to a critical value at the .01 level of 6.64.

6. The test statistic was 1.17 for the semi-log form and 2.70 for the linear form. Critical values are 1.44 and 1.69 at the .05 and .01 levels, respectively.

7. The appropriateness of pooling the data for oil-heated and gas-heated houses was tested by an F test. The value of the test statistic is 1.23; the critical value at the .01 level is 1.88.

8. Restriction of the sample to a compact neighborhood makes it

unnecessary to include variables for locational amenities in the hedonic price equation.

9. The sales data were obtained from the SREA Market Data Center, Inc., *Single Family Residential Sales* (Seattle, 1970 through 1975).

10. The estimated coefficient of a dummy variable, α, is equal (before multiplication by 100) to $\ln(1 + d)$, where d is the estimated relative effect on price. The percentage change is calculated as $100 \ (e^{\alpha} - 1)$. For further discussion, see Halvorsen and Palmquist (1980).

**Part III
The Choice of
Residential Location**

5

A Multinomial Logit Model of Residential Choice: Background and Theoretical Framework

In choosing a residential location, a household is making decisions along several dimensions: tenure, location, structure type, and neighborhood and community type. The purpose of this chapter is to present the locational choice component of a general decision model of intrametropolitan residential choice. This model takes into account the many dimensions of the choice problem and is empirically estimable, employing data on residential choices actually made by households in a metropolitan area.

Households are forced by the spatial nature of the choice of residential location to reveal their preferences for the economic determinants of residential choice in the metropolitan area. The work presented in this chapter and in chapter 6 thus takes advantage of the spatial dimension of the metropolitan economy to provide an economic test of the factors considered important by households in choosing a residential location and of how the relative importance of these factors varies among households of different types.

This choice is clearly a discrete one: a household faces all-or-nothing types of alternatives. In choosing a subarea of the metropolitan area in which to locate, a household must make a single choice among a relatively small set of mutually exclusive alternatives. In addition, as in the case of choice of occupation, the choice made has important implications for future well-being and is based in part on considerations of future contingencies. Once a locational choice is made, substantial costs are associated with altering that choice.

The results of estimating the model presented here describe how the distribution of choices by households is related to household characteristics and characteristics of potential residential choices; these results represent a step toward predicting the effects on urban spatial structure of public policies that alter either characteristics of locational choices or characteristics of households. Results such as those presented in chapter 6 can be used, for example, to predict the effects of policy changes that lead to income changes or changes in commuting costs. Economic theory predicts responses to such policy changes that vary across households, and the empirical results obtained can be used to test these implications.

The general decision model of which the work presented here is a component is a decision tree. Assuming place of employment as given, we assume that a household follows the following decision tree: first, a tenure choice is made; then, one of several locations or subareas of the metropolitan area is chosen; and finally, a bundle of housing services within the subarea is chosen, where this bundle includes not only the attributes of the actual structure but also the quality of the neighborhood and local public services. In this residential choice situation, in which the feasible choice set faced by a household is large, examining these component decisions separately has a number of advantages. Studies of decision behavior have found that choosers facing a large number of alternatives will attempt to minimize decision costs by simplifying the decision-making process in such a manner. In addition, there are certain unique aspects of each of the component decisions. Finally, this approach affords a good deal of computational convenience. Thus, at each stage of the decision problem, we assume that the household maximizes a utility function defined over the relevant alternatives. Given the nature of the choice problem, a multinomial logit model is employed to represent the decision process.

In what follows, several relevant background studies of residential choice and housing demand are reviewed first. Next, the model of choice of residential location is presented. Chapter 6 presents the data set and the empirical results.

Background

Several recent studies of residential choice and of housing demand in a spatial setting have introduced methodological innovations that provide important background to the work presented in this chapter and in chapter 6. The issues addressed by these studies include modeling the search process for housing or location, specifying intrametropolitan price variation for housing or location, taking into account the many dimensions of the housing-location package, appropriately accounting for cost or price variations introduced by the work trip, and selecting an appropriate statistical model. Although the list of studies discussed here is by no means comprehensive, these studies do highlight the types of methodological innovations that are of interest here.[1]

Straszheim's (1973, 1975) study of housing markets in the San Francisco-Bay Area is one of the earliest attempts to incorporate a variety of dimensions of the housing bundle into an empirical analysis and to allow the implicit prices for each of those dimensions to vary across locations within the metropolitan area. Straszheim employs a model that is an extension of the seminal work of Alonso (1964), in which households maximize a utility function that includes housing services, distance to work, and all other goods. If households have identical incomes and tastes and all household heads work at a single employment center, the market-clearing set of housing prices would form a negatively sloped housing price gradient with its peak at the single employment center. Straszheim extends the Alonso's framework by allowing household tastes to vary, by allowing household heads to work at locations other than the peak of the housing price gradient, and by allowing housing services to be a multidimensional commodity. Straszheim employs his model not to analyze residential location choice but as a means of constructing a spatially indexed measure of the market prices of housing facing households with heads working at different locations within the metropolitan area. Use of a procedure of this type is necessary because housing prices must vary before price elasticities of demand for housing can be estimated. If estimated price elasticities are to reflect how housesholds alter the quantity of housing consumed in response to variations in prices, the measure of housing prices must not reflect variations in housing services as well.

Straszheim's framework recognizes that some characteristics of a multidimensional housing bundle cannot vary continuously. Tenure and structure type, for instance, pose discrete rather than continuous alternatives. Price gradients for each of these discrete choices can be constructed, however, which is precisely what Straszheim does. Then, by selecting a standard housing bundle within each of these discrete alternatives, and pricing it at a fixed distance down the housing price gradient from each household's worksite, housing price indices can be constructed, for each discrete alternative, that do not reflect variations in the composition or quantity of housing services. Since houschold heads are employed at a variety of worksites, however, there will be variation in the value of the price indices across households within the sample. As mentioned earlier, this price variation is very useful. The weakness in this method of obtaining prices is that it assumes that each household looks at a single set of prices, defined by the standardized bundle, at a fixed distance down the rent gradient from its worksite. This criticism is blunted when Straszheim estimates separate demand equations for each of sixteen life-cycle classes of households, defined by marital status, age of head of household, and number of children in the household. Although variations in household incomes should also alter the type of bundle sought, Straszheim does not stratify by income, since he means to estimate income elasticities of demand.

There is, however, one difficulty with Straszheim's price indices. Consider again how he constructs these indices. He first estimates short-run implicit market prices for each attribute of the housing bundle (number of rooms, structure age, lot size, structure condition) in each of seventy-three residential zones. Separate equations are estimated for owner and rental units. This allows him to capture residence zone-specific quasi-rents in these estimated coefficients. He then estimates the relationship between each of these coefficients and travel time from one of two primary employment nodes (San Francisco or Oakland) to the residence zone to which that coefficient applies. This relationship is assumed to be negative exponential. Thus, $P_{jk} = A_{ik}e^{B_{ik}T_{ij}}$ where P_{jk} is the estimated price (coefficient) for housing attribute k in residence zone j, T_{ij} is the transport time between gradient source i and residence zone j, and A_{ik} and B_{ik} are the parameters to be estimated describing the relationship between the hedonic price for housing attribute k and transport time from gradient source i.

The peculiarity in this is the assumption that the price of each housing attribute declines exponentially with increasing distance from the gradient source. This assumption is justified for land rents or housing prices, (Muth 1969, Mills 1972) but not for housing attributes. There is no obvious reason, for instance, why the price per room should decrease smoothly with increasing distance from downtown San Francisco or Oakland. Rooms can be built anywhere, unlike space, which is by nature in fixed supply at any particular location. Although quasi-rents may exist for particular locations, there is no plausible theoretical explanation of why quasi-rents should vary systematically with distance from a gradient source.

Straszheim uses this framework to estimate demand models for six different aspects of housing: tenure, number of rooms, structure age, lot size, travel time, and total expenditures. In each of these models, he estimates income and direct price elasticities of demand, and cross-price elasticities where possible. His use of spatial variation in prices, as well as his use of detailed spatially disaggregated information on each of these six aspects of the housing consumed by each member of his sample, makes these demand estimates both feasible and interesting. Straszheim was one of the first to attempt to estimate cross-price elasticities of demand for individual components of the housing bundle. It is not clear, however, how certain of his results should be interpreted. This is because his price indices for number of rooms, structure age, lot size, and travel time decline exponentially with distance from the gradient source. In the cases of tenure choice and total expenditures, however, the sale price variables consist of prices of standardized packages of housing. Thus, in these cases, the foregoing criticism does not apply; Straszheim's hedonic equation results for the seventy-three residence zones are used appropriately here to estimate the price variation of housing over space.

Straszheim's tenure choice model is not sufficiently developed to provide reliable results. The price variable he uses does not distinguish adequately between the consumption and investment aspects of the alternative tenure choices. Since owning can provide potentially large investment gains, which can be expected to vary spatially within a metropolitan area, this is an important distinction to incorporate into any model of tenure choice.

It should also be noted that Straszheim estimates each of his demand models, including the tenure choice model, for samples of households that he is willing to assume have homogeneous tastes. These samples are intended to reflect stages in the life cycle and are defined by marital status, sex and age of household head, and number of children. The regression model he employs assumes that all households within any one of these life-cycle groups have identical tastes, and that any variations in the sample are simply caused by random measurement errors. If you believe that tastes vary within each of these life-cycle groups, a stochastic model of tenure choice would provide a more appropriate representation of that choice process. Subsequent tenure choice analysts have taken advantage of the multinomial logit model and its counterparts to analyze this choice process. These newer models include deterministic elements but assume that there is an important stochastic element to such choice. Pollakowski (1981) treats both the consumption-investment issue and the need for a stochastic choice model.

Quigley (1976) constructs a model of housing demand in which housing bundles are the unit of choice. He first partitions rental housing into eighteen types. Taking worksites as given, he then assumes that, for each housing type, households search out the location which has the lowest gross price (contract rent plus commuting cost) and then choose among these eighteen least-cost options. He obtains his spatially varying housing prices in two steps. First, he estimates the average price for each of eighteen distinct housing bundles, defined in terms of size, age, and structure type, in each of fifty separate residence zones. He then estimates work-trip costs for each household, given its fixed worksite, to each zone. His estimates assume that households will select the least-cost alternative (when automobile and public transit are the two possibilities) and are estimated as the sum of out-of-pocket costs and worker's value of time spent on the commute trip. Workers are assumed to value travel time at their wage rates. Households then identify, for each housing bundle, the minimum gross price (the sum of the contract price and these commuting costs). This yields a unique price for each bundle for each household.[2]

Quigley assumes housing tenure as given and estimates his model for a large sample of Pittsburgh renters. He uses the multinomial logit model to estimate how the selection of a housing bundle depends on the housing prices discussed earlier. This is a particularly advantageous statistical model for his purposes since it conveniently incorporates information about the numerous choices that face each household. Further advantages of this model are discussed later in this chapter and in appendix G.

Since Quigley's definition of housing types is based on three structural variables, neighborhood quality and public service quality are not adequately taken into account. The result, one suspects, is that households in this model are choosing among dwelling units in locations where neighborhood quality and public service quality are low. King (1974) presents some interesting empirical results that are consistent with this observation.

Using the same data set that Quigley used, Williams (1979) extends Quigley's model by considering neighborhood quality as an important component of the housing bundle. He then adds to the logit model a set of dummy variables describing the average income in the census tract in which a housing bundle is located.

Friedman (1975) constructs a model of residential location choice in which the object of choice is a community. The emphasis of the study is the role of public services in this choice. Households are assumed to survey all the communities within their feasible set of communities and to select the community that maximizes an indirect utility function that includes local public services, the local property tax rate, neighborhood characteristics, commuting distance, and real housing services.

Friedman notes that, within a class of households, it may be reasonable to posit a probabilistic utility function over discrete choices. This allows him to employ a multinomial logit model to estimate the parameters of the utility function. This model allows the explanatory variables to vary across choices as well as across choosers. For each household, each of the characteristics of the choice varies across the nine communities. Furthermore, one of the independent variables, real housing services, varies across choosers as well, while the remaining four variables take on the same values for all choosers.

Friedman's housing services variable is very important for his analysis and thus deserves some discussion. All the other variables in the household's hypothesized utility function take on fixed values in each community for each household; that is, the household can select a community, but within any given community it cannot alter or select a preferred value for any of these variables (publicly provided services, local tax rate,[3] neighborhood characteristics,[4] distance to the household's fixed worksite). Housing services are subject to choice within any given community, making the identification of the relevant magnitude of these for each community an important methodological problem. Friedman identifies the relevant magnitude of real housing services as follows. First, he estimates housing expenditures as a function of household income, household size, and age of the household head for each of the nine communities. He uses these results to predict housing expenditures for each household in each community. This gives him nine predicted expenditure levels for each household. He then estimates hedonic price equations for each community in which the cost of a dwelling unit depends on its number of rooms, its age and whether the neighborhood is predominantly single-family houses. He uses these results to estimate the expenditures required in each community to buy a standardized housing bundle. Finally, he creates his real housing services variable by dividing the predicted expenditure levels for each household by the expenditures required to buy a standardized bundle in each community for each household. This yields a measure of the quantity of housing services demanded by a particular type of household in a particular community, given housing prices in that community.

Friedman finds that his housing services variable has the largest coefficient of any of his estimates. In fact, the other explanatory variables, including local public services, appear to have little or no effect on choice of community. This result may very well depend on the relationship between his housing services variable and the other explanatory variables. The community-specific characteristics that are represented by these other variables influence both the numerator and denominator of the housing services variable in unspecified ways. The possibility cannot be ruled out that this variable reflects differences in community character in some unspecified way and that its large coefficient estimate is the result of this relationship.

This ambiguity notwithstanding, Friedman's methodological contribution is important. His study was the first to use a multinomial logit model to examine choice of community, and it established several useful precedents in doing so. The structure of the model presented in this chapter and in chapter 6 is broadly similar to Friedman's, although a housing price index is used instead of a measure of housing services.

Lerman (1976) employs Washington, D.C., microdata to estimate a joint choice model of location, housing, automobile ownership, and mode to work that takes full advantage of the multinomial logit model. Members of the sample are allowed to face, on average, over 145 discrete alternatives, from which they select one. Households choose a housing bundle (defined as involving tenure and structure type) simultaneously with their choices of location (defined as including neighborhood quality, density, school quality, and neighborhood racial composition), work trip, automobile ownership, and spatial opportunities (defined as including accessibility to shopping and other nonwork destinations). Their choices are also allowed to reflect their own characteristics, including income, race, household size, and number of drivers.

All costs are collapsed into one variable, which measures the income remaining for the household's use after paying all the costs incurred by the choice made. Thus, housing, transportation, and automobile-ownership costs are added to taxes, and their sum is subtracted from household income to provide the overall measure of costs (more accurately, income net of costs).

Many of the variables hypothesized to determine a household's choice are measured at the level of the census tract, but the presence of a variable number of housing units within census tracts means that different census tracts will have different probabilities of being selected. To correct for this, Lerman includes the natural log of the number of housing units in the census tract as an explanatory variable and points out that a coefficient of one for this variable would be consistent with the assumptions of the logit model. That is, a coefficient of one would indicate that tracts were completely homogeneous (hence, alternatives were independent within a tract), while a coefficient of zero would indicate that alternatives within a tract were not independent of one another. (See McFadden (1978) for a demonstration that the coefficient of this variable indexes the degree of independence at the alternatives within a tract.)

A Model of Intrametropolitan Locational Choice

The advantages of multinomial logit model of residential choice have been alluded to frequently in the preceding discussion. This section presents a logit model of intrametropolitan locational choice. As discussed earlier, this model is the locational choice component of a general model of residential choice.

Assume that a utility-maximizing household has J locational alternatives (subareas of the metropolitan area) from which to choose and that each subarea can be described by a vector of observed attributes x_j. Furthermore, assume that each household can be described by a vector of observed attributes s. The household has the utility function

$$U = V(x,s,\epsilon) \tag{5.1}$$

where the stochastic term ϵ is a vector of random elements that reflects the distribution of tastes or unobserved variations in attributes x_j.

More specifically, assume that the utility function can be written as

$$U = V(x,s) + \epsilon(x,s) \tag{5.2}$$

where V is nonstochastic and reflects the representative tastes of the population, and where we assume that the utility function has an additive stochastic term.

The probability that a given household will choose location i is given by

$$P_i = \text{Prob}[\, V(x_i,s) + \epsilon(x_i,s) > V(x_j,s) + \epsilon(x_j,s) \qquad \text{for all } j \neq i\,]$$

$$= \text{Prob}[\,\epsilon(x_j,s) - \epsilon(x_i,s) < V(x_i,s) - V(x_j,s) \qquad \text{for all } j \neq i\,] \qquad (5.3)$$

We must next specify the joint probability distribution for the random elements $\epsilon(x,s)$. Assume (1) that the odds that one subarea will be selected instead of another are independent of the absence or presence of other alternatives, (2) that all subareas have a positive selection probability for each household, and (3) that the determination of selection probabilities is additively separable in its arguments, representing the subarea effect and the household taste effect. Following McFadden (1974a, 1975), assume that the $\epsilon(x,s)$ are independent and identically distributed with the Weibell distribution

$$\text{Prob}[\,\epsilon(x_j,s) \leq \epsilon\,] = e^{-e^{-\epsilon}}. \qquad (5.4)$$

McFadden (1974a, 1975) has shown that we can then express the probability that a household will choose location i as

$$P_i = \frac{\exp[\, V(x_i,s)\,]}{\displaystyle\sum_{j=i}^{J} \exp[\, V(x_j,s)\,]}. \qquad (5.5)$$

The relative odds of choosing location i over location j thus satisfy

$$\log(P_i/P_j) = V(x_i,s) - V(x_j,s). \qquad (5.6)$$

In order to estimate equation 5.5, assume that the function $V(x,s)$ is linear in parameters. Thus,

$$V(x,s) = \sum_{k=1}^{K} \theta_k V^k(x,s).$$

We have N observations (s_n, B_n), where s_n is a vector of household characteristics and B_n is the feasible choice set of J locations. Each member of B_n has associated with it a vector of attributes x_{jn}. Let $Z_{jn}^k = V^k(x_{jn},s_n)$ and $Z_{jn} = (Z_{jn}^1, \ldots, Z_{jn}^K)$. Then equation 5.5 can be rewritten as[5]

$$P_{in} = P(x_{in}|s_n, B_n) = \frac{\exp(Z_{in}\theta)}{\sum_{j=1}^{J_n} \exp(Z_{jn}\theta)}. \tag{5.7}$$

Equation 5.7 is estimated as follows. The total sample is divided into sub-samples based on the household characteristics s. This allows us to examine the effects of locational characteristics, as perceived by households making locational decisions, on locational choice and to examine the manner in which these effects vary across households.

The relevant parameter estimates are obtained by maximum-likelihood techniques. Given that the utility function is linear in parameters, it can be demonstrated that the likelihood function is concave (McFadden 1974a). Iterative estimation techniques can thus be employed to find a unique maximum likelihood estimate of θ. McFadden has shown that the maximum-likelihood estimates of the parameters are consistent and asymptotically normal under quite general conditions.

Concluding Comments

The literature review in this chapter highlights five crucial issues that must be addressed when constructing an econometric model of intrametropolitan residential location choice. The model estimated in the following chapter takes advantage of recent methodological advances and a rich microdata set to appropriately respond to each of these issues. The issue of how to model the search process is addressed by assuming that it follows a decision-tree structure in which a tenure choice is made first,[6] followed by a location choice and a housing bundle choice. The second issue—the specification of intrametropolitan housing price variation—is handled in the following chapter by estimating and using hedonic price equations to construct the housing price variable. The third issue—appropriately accounting for the multiple dimensions of the housing-location bundle—is addressed by estimating the locational choice component of a general decision model of residential choice, employing prices that are standardized for neighborhood and structural differences over space. The fourth issue—appropriately accounting for work trip costs—is addressed by explicitly including a measure of travel time to the work site in the locational choice model. Measures of housing availability and employment accessibility are also included to capture the effects of both current search costs and possible future search and moving costs on location choice. Finally, the fifth issue—choice of an appropriate statistical model—is resolved by using the multinomial logit model described in this chapter. The multinomial logit model provides a tractable statistical model of how individuals select one alternative from a number of discrete alternatives, which is precisely the situation that confronts a household searching for a residential location. A detailed discussion of its assumptions, derivation, and certain of its important features is contained in appendix G.

Notes

1. Additional relevant empirical work relating to residential choice or housing demand in a spatial setting includes Diamond (1975), Ellickson (1981), Ingram, *et al.* (1972), King (1976), Leven and Mark (1977), Mayo (1975), Reschovsky (1979), Segal (1979), Siegel (1975), Weinberg (1978), Weisbrod (1978), and Weisbrod, Lerman, and Ben-Akiva (1980). Also see the relevant contributions and discussion in Ingram (1977).

2. Quigley actually employs the average of the lowest 5 percent of the total prices for each bundle and household, on the grounds that search costs may prevent households from locating the lowest possible price for each bundle.

3. This is not strictly true for local taxes, which really is the relevant variable, since the household can vary its property tax burden by varying the quantity of housing it chooses (that is, by varying Q) or by altering its tenure choice if any portion of property taxes is capitalized.

4. Neighborhood characteristics certainly do vary within a given local political jurisdiction; assuming this away is merely a means of simplifying the econometrics.

5. See McFadden (1974*a*).

6. Pollakowski (1981) examines tenure choice in a spatial setting.

6

The Multinomial Logit Model: Sample and Empirical Results

This chapter describes the estimation of the multinomial logit model of residential choice presented in chapter 5. First, the sample is presented. Next, the variables used to represent the distinguishing locational characteristics are described. This is followed by presentation and discussion of the empirical results.

The Sample

Data for the San Francisco Bay Area were employed to estimate the model. This metropolitan area is very suitable for this purpose in many ways. It is large and diverse and contains subareas with distinct characteristics. There are distinct differences, for example, between the central cities of San Francisco and Oakland. There are also suburban areas of varying character located at different distances from the city of San Francisco. In addition, the unique topography of the Bay Area facilities the definition of distinct subareas. San Francisco is bordered by water on all sides except its southern boundary. The communities of Marin County also form a distinctly defined subarea; residents have to cross at least one bridge to reach any large concentration of employment. The communities in the Contra Costa subarca lie to the east of a mountain ridge that separates them from the remainder of the urbanized portion of the Bay Area.

The feasible choice set of subareas is listed and defined in table 6-1. Several factors were considered in defining this choice set. The sample chosen consisted of households whose primary worker was employed in the extended San Francisco central business district (CBD). In order to specify the feasible choice set of locations facing a San Francisco CBD worker, the locational distribution of these workers was examined first. The subareas were thus chosen with the aim of including the communities in which a substantial share of San Francisco CBD workers lived while defining reasonably distinct geographical subareas. In general, the set of communities constituting the subareas was made up of those in which one percent or more of the San Francisco CBD workers resided, plus selected other communities that appeared to be equally likely choices, since they were similar to those

Table 6–1
Definitions of Locations

Location	Cities
1. San Francisco	San Francisco
2. Oakland	Oakland
3. Contra Costa County	Lafayette
	Walnut Creek
	Pleasant Hill
	Concord
4. Marin County	Mill Valley
	San Anselmo
	San Rafael
	Fairfax
	Ross
	Costa Maderara
	Larkspur
5. Berkeley	El Cerrito
	Albany
	Berkeley
	Piedmont
	Kensington
6. North San Mateo County	Daly City
	Colma
	Brisbana
	South San Francisco
7. Central San Mateo County	San Bruno
	Millbrae
	Burlingame
	San Mateo
	Millsborough
8. South San Mateo County	Belmont
	San Carlos
	Redwood City
	Atherton
	Menlo Park
	Woodside

that were chosen. Several small communities were excluded on the grounds either that they were chiefly resort communities or that they would have made the subareas less geographically compact than was desirable. Rural areas and small unincorporated areas were also excluded for the same reasons and because they invariably were rarely chosen as residence areas. Table 6–2, which summerizes commuting patterns for the San Francisco CBD, reflects the importance of the chosen subareas.

The data employed are primarily drawn from a random sample of approximately 29,000 households collected in 1965 for the Bay Area Trans-

Table 6-2
Weekday Home-Based Work Trips to or from San Francisco Central Business District

Location	Number of Trips	Percentage
San Francisco	261,542	61.1
Oakland[a]	25,746	6.0
Contra Costa[a]	9,854	2.3
Marin[b]	26,927	6.3
Berkeley[b]	20,550	4.8
North San Mateo County[a]	35,257	8.2
Central San Mateo County[a]	13,361	3.1
South San Mateo Country[a]	11,837	2.8
Other	23,250	5.4
Total	428,324	100.0

Source: BATSC, *Average Weekday Trips Between Superdistricts* (1965).
Note: The San Francisco CBD is approximated by BATSC Superdistrict No. 1.
[a]Numbers are for BATSC superdistricts that are approximately equivalent to the subarea location.
[b]Numbers are for BATSC superdistricts that are unavoidably larger than the subarea location.

portation Study Commission. This home interview survey data set, also employed in chapter 2, provides individual household information regarding household demographic characteristics, household income, job location, occupation and industry in which the household's primary worker is employed, residential location, a description of the household's dwelling unit, and some information on the character of the immediate neighborhood in which the dwelling unit is located. These data have been supplemented by other data that describe more completely the economic characteristics of the household's feasible choice set of potential locational choices. Table 6-3 presents the variables employed and the sources of data. Table 6-4 presents the distribution of households of San Francisco CBD workers across residence zones and by demographic characteristics.

The Locational Characteristics

The locational characteristics were chosen in an attempt to best represent the factors that a household whose primary worker was employed in the extended San Francisco CBD perceived as the most important distinguishing characteristics of any particular area in the larger metropolitan area. These factors include both measures of relative locational costs and measures of qualitative aspects of areas. In addition to including commuting

Table 6–3
Definitions and Sources of Variables

Variable	Definition and Source
Location characteristics	
Relative housing price	Predicted relative housing price (in thousands of dollars; see text and tables 6–5 and 6–6)
Travel time	Travel time from San Francisco CBD (hours) (2)
Housing availability index	Percentage of units in one of three price classes; corresponds to chooser income (see text and (1))
Employment accessibility index	Gravity index of work site availability (see text and (2)(3))

Data sources are as follows
(1) U.S. Bureau of the Census, *Census of Housing, 1960,* 1963.
(2) Bay Area Simulation Study, 1968.
(3) Bay Area Transportation Study Commission, *Employment Inventory,* 1964.

costs and housing prices, the key signals in standard theories of residential choice, attention is also directed to other economic factors of interest, especially search costs and expected moving costs.

The relative price of any given bundle of structural and neighborhood attributes will be of primary importance in choosing a residential location. Although different households will prefer different bundles of attributes, and although households will substitute among attributes across areas, it is nevertheless true that it is relatively more costly to locate in some areas than it is in others. An index of relative housing prices has thus been created as follows. For each area, the estimated market value of dwelling units was regressed on a set of structural and neighborhood variables describing the dwelling units.[1] This procedure yielded a set of hedonic price-predicting equations. Next, for each of nine income-household size classes constituting the sample of households whose primary worker was employed in the San Francisco CBD, the mean bundle of attributes purchased was computed. The price of this bundle was then computed for each income-household size class for each area by use of the price-predicting equations. The regression results and the definitions of the variables employed are presented in tables 6–5 and 6–6. Table 6–7 displays the predicted prices.

The cost of commuting to work in the San Francisco CBD will also be of primary importance in choosing a residential location. Other things being equal, households will attempt to minimize travel cost. Thus, the driving time from the San Francisco CBD to a typical point in the area is employed as an explanatory variable. The assumption is that driving times and money costs of commuting are highly correlated. The fact that the time cost of any given work trip will vary among workers depending on how they value com-

Table 6-4
Distribution of Households with Head of Household Employed in San Francisco CBD, by Location, Income, Household Size, and Age of Household Head

Location	Total Number of Households	Income			Household Size			Age of Household Head					
		≤ $9,500	$9,500–$13,750	>$13,750	≤2	3–4	≥5	≤25	25–35	35–45	45–55	55–65	>65
San Francisco	348	166	111	71	149	133	66	5	36	83	111	94	19
Oakland	74	30	22	22	36	29	9	0	7	20	22	22	3
Contra Costa County	114	47	48	19	16	61	35	1	42	40	23	7	1
Marin County	108	32	35	41	32	50	26	2	18	36	35	14	3
Berkeley	98	17	33	48	22	55	21	0	6	26	38	22	6
North San Mateo County	169	93	59	17	33	83	53	7	41	59	38	23	1
Central San Mateo County	193	66	56	71	43	103	47	4	34	62	53	34	6
South San Mateo County	103	19	36	48	29	50	24	2	6	40	31	23	1

Table 6-5
Price-Predicting Regressions for Single-Family Owner-Occupied Dwellings

Variable	I	II	III	IV	V	VI	VII	VIII
Constant	−9.62	−15.0	−5.74	−4.45	−15.7	9.32	−2.18	−2.36
	(4.96)	(2.72)	(5.30)	(10.1)	(9.48)	(9.53)	(5.35)	(8.23)
MEDINC	.00259	.00270	.00236	.00460	.00124	−.00147	.00148	.001?
	(.000278)	(.000313)	(.000338)	(.000829)	(.000238)	(.000957)	(.000139)	(.000?
DEN	−39.1	1.80	−30.9	−65.5	−84.7	−57.8	−99.3	−72.1
	(7.97)	(5.88)	(11.0)	(55.3)	(40.2)	(18.7)	(13.2)	(17.3)
NRMS	3.58	2.31	2.86	3.59	3.20	2.75	3.15	2.38
	(.252)	(.188)	(.268)	(.359)	(.294)	(.370)	(.231)	(.295)
DAA	10.3	7.51	3.89	7.76	15.0	5.10	6.89	12.2
	(1.65)	(1.36)	(.864)	(1.60)	(3.06)	(1.04)	(1.30)	(1.44)
DAB	5.19	5.64	1.71	4.96	6.67	1.28	3.10	6.73
	(1.11)	(.933)	(.729)	(1.35)	(1.37)	(.793)	(.793)	(.947)
DC	11.0	3.00	6.55	21.8	15.0	8.20	−1.03	−2.48
	(4.01)	(1.83)	(3.75)	(4.29)	(6.63)	(6.17)	(4.84)	(6.49)
DNA	.786	.158	−8.22	−28.1	−.660	3.69	7.99	8.98
	(1.22)	(1.22)	(3.38)	(6.11)	(14.78)	(2.17)	(2.49)	(5.30)
LOT	12.3	14.4	11.9	16.6	19.8	10.5	7.07	17.6
	(3.37)	(1.69)	(11.6)	(1.90)	(3.36)	(2.89)	(1.74)	(1.82)
PCTOO	−16.4	−3.15	−8.40	−30.4	−4.35	1.88	−5.53	−4.39
	(2.14)	(2.35)	(3.28)	(6.76)	(6.03)	(2.86)	(2.42)	(2.74)
$\bar{R}^2$	.452	.530	.501	.549	.639	.288	.712	.720
N	794	915	673	315	288	377	637	460

Columns are I, San Francisco; II, Oakland; III, Contra Costa County; IV, Marin County; V, Berkeley; VI, North San Mateo County; VII, Central San Mateo County; VIII, South San Mateo County. Left-hand variable is market value, in thousands of dollars.

muting time is partially accounted for by estimating the model for different income classes.

Search costs associated with locating in any given area within the larger metropolitan area are also likely to influence locational choice. It is thus important to consider the composition of the housing stock in each area. The less available housing is in a given price range, the more costly it is to search for housing in that area. There is relatively more low-income housing available in Oakland, for example, than in the Contra Costa area. Thus, an index of the availability of housing in a given area in the price range most likely to be considered by the household in question is employed. The availability index was constructed as follows. The housing stock was divided into three categories, based on value. These categories were chosen to correspond roughly to the value ranges in which each of the three income classes employed here would be likely to purchase. The index of availability for each income class was thus computed as the proportion of the housing in each area in its corresponding price range.

Table 6-6
Definitions of Variables Employed in Price-Predicting Equation for Single-Family Owner-Occupied Dwellings

Variable	Definition and Source
Left-hand variable	
VALUE	Property value, in thousands of dollars (2)
Right-hand variable	
MEDINC	Median income in relevant census tract (1)
DEN	Percentage of units in relevant census tract with more than one person per room (1)
NRMS	Rooms in housing unit (2)
DAA	D = 1 if dwelling unit built 1960–1965 (2)
DAB	D = 1 if dwelling unit built 1950–1959 (2)
DC	D = 1 if dwelling unit sound and regularly maintained (2)
DNA	D = 1 if predominantly single-family neighborhood type (2)
LOT	Lot size in acres
PCTOO	Percentage of owner-occupied units in relevant census tract (1)

Sources: (1) 1960 Census of Population and Census of Housing; (2) Bay Area Transportation Study Commission, 1965.

Another locational characteristic of interest is an index of accessibility to all jobs in the Bay Area. Relative proximity to places of employment other than in the San Francisco CBD may be important to households for a number of reasons. Since searching for and subsequently moving to a new residential location is quite costly, a household will presumably consider future contingencies in making its choice. More specifically, although the worksite of the primary household worker is taken as given here, households will presumably act to minimize expected moving costs by taking into account possibilities of job relocation and job opportunities for secondary household workers. Large numbers of households have two or more workers, and the nonprimary workers often have temporary jobs. In addition, residing in an area that is proximate to a large number of jobs lowers the transitional costs incurred by the household in the event that the primary worker chooses to be employed someplace other than in the San Francisco CBD. Proximity to additional employment sites lowers the likelihood of the household's choosing to relocate in the event of a change in job location for the primary worker, and thereby decreases the expected costs to the household of such a job change. The household is thus seen as buying insurance against future employment contingencies by locating near other jobs. It should be noted that, by considering future contingencies, we are deviat-

Table 6–7
Predicted Prices of Single-Family Owner-Occupied Standardized Housing Bundles, by Income, Household Size, and Location

Location	Household Size		
	≤ 2	3–4	> 4
Income ≤ $9,500			
San Francisco	$34,700	$35,100	$36,300
Oakland	28,200	29,200	30,700
Contra Costa County	25,300	25,900	27,100
Marin County	28,800	29,300	31,100
Berkeley	29,600	30,100	31,500
North San Mateo County	28,900	28,800	29,300
Central San Mateo County	26,300	26,400	26,900
South San Mateo County	31,200	31,700	33,000
Income $9,500–$13,750			
San Francisco	$39,500	$39,900	$36,300
Oakland	33,600	34,300	30,800
Contra Costa County	30,100	30,600	27,100
Marin County	35,900	36,300	31,200
Berkeley	35,800	36,100	31,600
North San Mateo County	30,900	30,700	29,300
Central San Mateo County	30,100	30,500	26,600
South San Mateo County	36,800	37,100	33,100
Income > $13,750			
San Francisco	$40,900	$41,400	$37,900
Oakland	34,400	35,300	34,200
Contra Costa County	31,000	31,800	29,400
Marin County	38,300	38,300	32,400
Berkeley	36,800	38,400	35,600
North San Mateo County	31,000	32,400	31,500
Central San Mateo County	30,800	31,800	28,200
South San Mateo County	37,800	39,000	36,600

ing from the frequently employed assumption that, work sites given, residential sites are allocated to households costlessly in a periodic auction.

The employment accessibility index used in chapter 2 is used here. Each census tract is assigned an index value equal to

$$\sum_j \frac{E_j}{(d_j)^2}$$

where E_j is total employment in the jth census tract, d_j is free-flow driving time from the census tract in question to the jth census tract, and the summation is done over all census tracts except the one in question. Appendix B describes the data used to construct this index.

Table 6-8
Maximum-Likelihood Coefficient Estimates, by Income Class

	Income Class		
	≤ $9,500	$9,500–$13,750	> $13,750
Relative housing price	− .228	− .0515	.0175
(in thousands of dollars)	(.0357)	(.0257)	(.0110)
Travel time to San Francisco CBD	− .00202	.0138	− .00705
	(.00492)	(.00537)	(.00808)
Housing availability index	− 2.38	2.57	3.64
	(.472)	(0.713)	(0.723)
Employment accessibility index[a]	.686	.454	.0721
	(.0988)	(.0961)	(.128)
Number of observations	470	400	337
Maximum log likelihood	− 862.3	− 793.9	− 671.6
Log likelihood for $\theta = 0$	− 977.3	− 831.8	− 700.8

Numbers in parentheses are asymptotic standard errors.
[a]The coefficient estimates for the employment accessibility index are multiplied by 1000 for presentation here.

Empirical Results

In this section, empirical results are presented for owner-occupant households. The sample consists of households in the Bay Area Transportation Study Commission data set whose principal worker is white and is employed in the extended San Francisco CBD.

Table 6-8 presents maximum-likelihood parameter estimates of the effects of the location-specific variables on intrametropolitan residential choice. Results are presented for three household income classes. The parameter estimate of the relative housing price variable takes the anticipated negative sign in two out of three cases, and the importance of housing price declines with household income.

The results for the travel time variable are difficult to interpret. Commuting cost has the expected negative effect on locational choice for the lowest and highest income groups, but the coefficient estimates are not statistically significant. For the middle income class, however, an unanticipated positive and statistically significant coefficient estimate is obtained. It is possible that the absence of an explicit value of time measure has led to these mixed results.

The parameter estimates for the housing availability index indicate that the highest two income classes are attracted to neighborhoods having greater proportions of housing in the value range most likely to be considered by households in these classes, whereas this is not the case for the lowest income class. This result is consistent with higher-income households being more concerned about search costs, given that they value their time more highly.[2]

The employment accessibility coefficient takes the expected positive sign in all cases, although it is small and statistically insignificant for the highest income class. The finding that the importance of employment accessibility decreases as income rises suggests that lower-income households may face more uncertain employment tenure prospects, may rely more on secondary wage earners, or may simply be more risk-averse than higher-income households.

Concluding Comments

In this chapter a multinomial logit model has been employed to examine choice of residential location in the San Francisco Bay Area. Results have been obtained which underscore the importance of relative housing prices, search costs, and expected search or moving costs to this choice. The results of estimating models such as this one represent an important step toward accurately assessing the residential location consequences of public policies that alter either characteristics of locational choices or characteristics of households. This is clearly a promising area for continued work.[3]

Notes

1. In further work, levels of local public service quality and property taxes should be included in this equation.

2. It should be noted, however, that this result is also consistent with the hypothesis that households prefer higher quality neighborhoods, as measured by neighborhood housing values. Although several variables in the hedonic price-predicting equations were intended to control for neighborhood quality, it is possible that some aspects of neighborhood quality were not adequately accounted for. The omission of public service and tax variables from the price-predicting equations could also have led to this result.

3. See, for example, Pollakowski (1981) (housing tenure choice) and Lerman, Pollakowski, and Segal (1981) (innercity neighborhood choice).

Appendix A:
Choice of Functional
Form for Hedonic
Price Equations

Hedonic price equations were used as the primary methodological tool in chapters 1 through 4, and as a supporting tool in chapters 5 and 6. The functional forms employed have been linear and semi-log. It was suggested in the text that future work in this area should more seriously consider the choice of functional form. This appendix provides a framework within which this choice can be made.

A hedonic price equation is a reduced-form equation reflecting both supply and demand influences. Therefore, the appropriate functional form for the hedonic price equation cannot generally be specified on theoretical grounds.[1] In practice, the choice of functional form has usually been based mainly on considerations of convenience in dealing with the problem at hand. Although reference has sometimes been made to experimentation with respect to the goodness of fit of alternative forms, the comparison of goodness of fit has generally not been embedded in a relevant statistical framework. Also, the range of forms considered has been limited to forms that place severe restrictions on the underlying demand and supply functions, including nonjointness in both consumption and production.[2]

Griliches (1967) drew attention to an article by Box and Cox (1964) that provided an appropriate methodology for choosing among functional forms. Although the Box-Cox methodology has received considerable use in other applications,[3] it has only recently been applied in hedonic studies (see, for example, Goodman 1978, Linneman 1980, Sonstelie and Portney 1980). These recent applications, however, only consider forms that impose highly restrictive assumptions on the underlying demand and supply functions.

One way to avoid the imposition of theoretical unwarranted restrictions is to use a flexible functional form.[4] This approach has been used extensively in other applications,[5] but it has not been used in studies employing

This appendix is based on Robert Halvorsen and Henry O. Pollakowski, "Choice of Functional Form for Hedonic Price Equations," *Journal of Urban Economics* 10 (July 1981): 37–49. Copyright © 1981 by Academic Press, Inc. Used with permission.

hedonic price equations. Although the use of flexible functional forms would eliminate the problem of using an overly restrictive form, the question of which flexible form to use would remain, as would the question of which restrictions, if any, were in fact warranted.

In this appendix, a procedure is proposed for choice of functional form for hedonic price equations that combines the best features of the Box-Cox and flexible functional form approaches.[6] A highly general functional form is specified, which yields all other functional forms of interest as special cases. Likelihood-ratio tests are then used to test the appropriateness of alternative functional forms of the hedonic equations. The application of this procedure is illustrated by the estimation of a hedonic price equation for housing with cross-section microdata.

The Model

The general functional form that incorporates all other functional forms of interest as special cases is

$$P^{(\theta)} = \alpha_0 + \sum_{i=1}^{m} \alpha_i Z_i^{(\lambda)} + \frac{1}{2} \sum_{i=1}^{m} \sum_{j=1}^{m} \gamma_{ij} Z_i^{(\lambda)} Z_j^{(\lambda)} \tag{A.1}$$

where P is price, the Z_i are attributes, $\gamma_{ij} = \gamma_{ji}$,[7] and $P^{(\theta)}$ and $Z^{(\lambda)}$ are Box-Cox transformations,[8]

$$P^{(\theta)} = \begin{cases} (P^\theta - 1)/\theta & \theta \neq 0 \\ \ln P & \theta = 0 \end{cases}$$

$$Z_i^{(\lambda)} = \begin{cases} (Z_i^\lambda - 1)/\lambda & \lambda \neq 0 \\ \ln Z_i & \lambda = 0 \end{cases}$$

The transformations are continuous around $\theta = 0$ and $\lambda = 0$, since the limit for the $\theta \neq 0$ case as $\theta \to 0$ is $\ln P$ and the limit for the $\lambda \neq 0$ case as $\lambda \to 0$ is $\ln Z_i$. Equation A.1 will be referred to as the quadratic Box-Cox functional form.[9]

The translog form (Christensen, Jorgenson, and Lau 1971, 1973),

$$\ln P = \alpha_0 + \sum_i \alpha_i \ln Z_i + \frac{1}{2} \sum_i \sum_j \gamma_{ij} \ln Z_i \ln Z_j$$

is obtained from the quadratic Box-Cox form by imposing the restrictions

$\theta = 0$ and $\lambda = 0$. The log-linear form is obtained as a special case of the translog form by imposing the further restrictions $\gamma_{ij} = 0$ for all i, j.

To facilitate the derivation of other functional forms, equation A.1 is rewritten:

$$P = \left\{ 1 + \theta \left[\alpha_0 + \sum_i \alpha_i \left(\frac{Z_i^\lambda - 1}{\lambda} \right) \right. \right.$$

$$\left. \left. + \frac{1}{2} \sum_i \sum_j \gamma_{ij} \left(\frac{Z_i^\lambda - 1}{\lambda} \right) \left(\frac{Z_j^\lambda - 1}{\lambda} \right) \right] \right\}^{1 \backslash \theta}. \tag{A.2}$$

Imposing the restrictions $\theta = \lambda = 1$ in equation A.2 yields the quadratic form (Lau 1974)

$$P = c_0 + \sum_i c_i Z_i + \sum_i \sum_j \gamma_{ij} Z_i Z_j \tag{A.3}$$

where

$$c_0 = 1 + \alpha_0 - \sum_i \left(\alpha_i - \frac{1}{2} \sum_j \gamma_{ij} \right)$$

$$c_i = \alpha_i - \sum_j \gamma_{ij}$$

The linear form can be obtained from the quadratic form by imposing the restrictions $\gamma_{ij} = 0$ for all i, j, in equation A.3.

The generalized square-root quadratic form[10] is obtained by imposing the restrictions $\theta = 2$, $\lambda = 1$ in equation A.2,

$$P = \left(b_0 + \sum_i b_i Z_i + \sum_i \sum_j \gamma_{ij} Z_i Z_j \right)^{1/2} \tag{A.4}$$

where

$$b_0 = 1 + 2\alpha_0 - \sum_i \left(2\alpha_i - \sum_j \gamma_{ij} \right)$$

$$b_i = 2 \left(\alpha_i - \sum_j \gamma_{ij} \right)$$

The square-root quadratic form (Diewert 1974),

$$P = \left(\sum_i \sum_j \gamma_{ij} Z_i Z_j \right)^{1/2} \tag{A.5}$$

is obtained by imposing the restrictions $b_0 = b_i = 0$ in equation A.4.[11]

A generalized nonhomogenous version of the generalized Leontief form (Diewert 1971) is obtained by imposing the restrictions $\theta = 1$, $\lambda = 1/2$ in equation A.2,

$$P = a_0 + \sum_i a_i Z_i^{\frac{1}{2}} + 2\sum_i \sum_j \gamma_{ij} Z_i^{\frac{1}{2}} Z_j^{\frac{1}{2}} \tag{A.6}$$

where

$$a_0 = 1 + \alpha_0 - 2\sum_i \left(\alpha_i - \sum_j \gamma_{ij}\right)$$

$$a_i = 2\left(\alpha_i - 2\sum_j \gamma_{ij}\right).$$

A linear homogeneous version of the generalized Leontief form

$$P = 2\sum_i \sum_j \gamma_{ij} Z_i^{\frac{1}{2}} Z_j^{\frac{1}{2}} \tag{A.7}$$

is obtained by imposing the restrictions $a_0 = a_i = 0$ in equation A.8.[12] The linear form can be obtained from equation A.6 by imposing the restrictions $a_i = 0$ and $\gamma_{ij} = 0$, $i \neq j$.

A functional form frequently used in previous studies of hedonic price equations is the semi-log form,

$$\ln P = d_0 + \sum_i d_i Z_i$$

The semi-log form is obtained as a special case of the quadratic Box-Cox functional form by imposing the restrictions $\theta = 0$, $\lambda = 1$, and $\gamma_{ij} = 0$ for all i, j.

In order to test whether a particular functional form is appropriate, the restrictions corresponding to that functional form are tested, using a likelihood-ratio test. Estimation and testing procedures are discussed in the next section.

Estimation Procedures[13]

Including a stochastic disturbance term in equation A.1, the equation to be estimated is

$$P_k^{(\theta)} = \alpha_0 + \sum_{i=1}^{m} \alpha_i Z_{ki}^{(\lambda)} + \frac{1}{2} \sum_{i=1}^{m} \sum_{j=1}^{m} \gamma_{ij} Z_{ki}^{(\lambda)} Z_{kj}^{(\lambda)} + \epsilon_k \qquad \text{(A.8)}$$

where $P_k^{(\theta)}$ is the kth observation on the transformed price variable; $Z_{ki}^{(\lambda)}$ is the kth observation on the transformed attribute i; θ, λ, α_0, α_i, and γ_{ij} are unknown parameters; and ϵ_k is the disturbance term. It is assumed that, for the true functional form (the true θ and λ), the disturbance term is normally and independently distributed with zero mean and constant variance.

Under the assumption of normality, the probability-density function for the transformed dependent variable may be written as

$$f(P_k^{(\theta)}) = (2\pi\sigma^2)^{\frac{1}{2}} \exp\left[-\frac{\left(\alpha_0 + \sum_i \alpha_i Z_{ki}^{(\lambda)} + \frac{1}{2} \sum_i \sum_j \gamma_{ij} Z_i^{(\lambda)} Z_j^{(\lambda)} \right)^2}{2\sigma^2} \right] \qquad \text{(A.9)}$$

The probability-density function for the untransformed dependent variable is

$$f(P_k) = f(P_k^{(\theta)}) J \qquad \text{(A.10)}$$

where J is the Jacobian of the inverse transformation from the transformed dependent variable to the actually observed dependent variable,

$$J = \left| \frac{dP_k^{(\theta)}}{dP_k} \right| = P_k^{\theta} - 1 \qquad \text{(A.11)}$$

The likelihood function for a sample of n observations on the untransformed dependent variable is the product of the density for each observation. Maximizing this function or its logarithm yields estimates of θ, λ, α_0, α_i, and γ_{ij}.

Ordinary least squares regression programs can be used to obtain the maximum-likelihood estimates. Note that, for a given θ and λ, equation A.8 is linear in the parameters α_0, α_i, and γ_{ij}. By a suitable redefinition of the variables, the equation can be rewritten in matrix form as

$$P^{(\theta)} = X\beta + \epsilon \qquad \text{(A.12)}$$

where X is the matrix

$$
\begin{bmatrix}
1 & Z_{11}^{(\lambda)} & \dots & Z_{1m}^{(\lambda)} & Z_{11}^{(\lambda)} \cdot Z_{11}^{(\lambda)} & \dots & Z_{1m}^{(\lambda)} \cdot Z_{1m}^{(\lambda)} \\
& \vdots & & \vdots & \vdots & & \vdots \\
1 & Z_{n1}^{(\lambda)} & \dots & Z_{nm}^{(\lambda)} & Z_{n1}^{(\lambda)} \cdot Z_{n1}^{(\lambda)} & \dots & Z_{nm}^{(\lambda)} \cdot Z_{nm}^{(\lambda)}
\end{bmatrix}
$$

and β is the column vector $[\alpha_0 \; \alpha_1 \dots \alpha_m \; \gamma_{11} \dots \gamma_{mm}$.

The likelihood function for a sample of n observations on the untransformed dependent variable may then be written as

$$
(2\pi\sigma)^{-n/2} \exp\left[\frac{[P^{(\theta)} - X\beta]'(P^{(\theta)} - X\beta)]}{2\sigma^2} \right] \prod_{k=1}^{n} P_k^{\theta-1} \tag{A.13}
$$

For a given θ and λ, equation A.13, except for a constant factor, is the likelihood for a standard least-squares problem. Therefore, the maximum-likelihood estimates of the β's are the ordinary least-squares estimates for the dependent variable $P^{(\theta)}$, and the estimate of σ^2 for a given θ and λ is

$$
\hat{\sigma}^2(\theta, \lambda) = \frac{\text{SSR}}{n}
$$

where SSR is the residual sum of squares.

Thus, for a fixed θ and λ, the maximized log likelihood, except for a constant, is

$$
L_{\max}(\theta, \lambda) = -\frac{n}{2} \ln \sigma^2(\theta, \lambda) + (\theta - 1) \sum_{k=1}^{n} \ln P_k \tag{A.14}
$$

where the second term is obtained from the Jacobian. To maximize over the entire parameter space, it is necessary only to estimate equation A.12 for alternative values for θ and λ and to find the values of θ and λ for which equation A.14 is maximized.

A test of whether a particular functional form is acceptable is performed by testing the null hypothesis that the parameters of the hedonic price equation satisfy the relevant restrictions. The hypothesis tests are based on the large sample theory result that, under the null hypothesis, twice the difference in the logarithmic likelihood between a null and an alternative hypothesis is distributed as X^2, with the number of degrees of freedom equal to the difference in the number of unrestricted parameters.

This result can also be used to form confidence regions around the estimates $(\hat{\theta}, \hat{\lambda})$ obtained using the unrestricted Box-Cox quadratic form. A

100 $(1 - \alpha)$ percent confidence region consists of all points (θ^*, λ^*) that satisfy the inequality

$$L_{\max}(\hat{\theta}, \hat{\lambda}) - L_{\max}(\theta^*, \lambda^*) < \frac{1}{2} \chi_2^2(\alpha).$$

For $\alpha = .01, \frac{1}{2} \chi_2^2 = 4.605$.

The translog, quadratic, generalized square-root quadratic, and non-homogenous version of the generalized Leontief functional forms involve restrictions on θ and λ only, and thus tests of these functional forms consist simply of determining whether the corresponding values (θ^*, λ^*) fall within the appropriate confidence region.

The semi-log form is also tested directly on the quadratic Box-Cox form. The log-linear form is tested conditional on acceptance of the translog form. The square-root quadratic form is tested conditional on acceptance of the generalized square-root quadratic form. The linear form is tested conditional on the quadratic form and on the generalized Leontief form. The linear homogeneous version of the generalized Leontief form is tested conditional on acceptance of the nonhomogeneous version.

Because the testing procedure is only partially nested, it will not generally indicate that there is one and only one acceptable functional form for a particular application. If more than one of the nonnested alternatives were accepted, the choice among them could be based on several criteria. First, it might be possible to apply a nonnested testing procedure; for example, Berndt, Darrough, and Diewert (1977) provide a Bayesian rationale for choosing among alternative flexible functional forms on the basis of the size of the log likelihood. Second, if the choice is narrowed to two or more of the standard hedonic forms (the linear, semi-log, and log-linear), there may be theoretical grounds for preferring one to another. Finally, in the absence of firm statistical or theoretical grounds for choosing among the acceptable functional forms, the choice can be based on convenience in dealing with the problem at hand.

Application

The use of the quadratic Box-Cox procedure for choice of the functional form for a hedonic price equation is illustrated by use of housing microdata drawn from the same sources that were used in chapters 2 and 6. The data set consists of a sample of 5,727 single-family owner-occupied dwelling units in the San Francisco Bay Area. The primary data source is the 1965

Bay Area Transportation Study Commission (BATSC) survey of about 29,000 households. The housing data from this survey are supplemented by data describing neighborhood characteristics and employment accessibility. The specific variables employed in this illustration are number of rooms, age, lot size, median income in census tract, median number of rooms in census tract, percentage of dwelling units in census tract that are owner-occupied, and an employment accessibility index.[14]

The alternative functional forms of the hedonic price equation are estimated using ordinary least squares. In estimating the unrestricted quadratic Box-Cox form, a grid search was performed over values of θ and λ between -1.0 and 2.0 in order to find the values of θ and λ that maximized the log likelihood. The optimum optimorum for the quadratic Box-Cox form was found to be $\theta = 0.06$, $\lambda = 0.28$. The parameter estimates are generally precise. Of the thirty-six parameters estimated, twenty-three are significant at the .01 level using two-tailed tests, and an additional three are significant at the .05 level.[15]

The 99 percent confidence region around $\theta = 0.06$, $\lambda = 0.28$ is shown in figure A–1. As indicated by the shape of the confidence region, the value

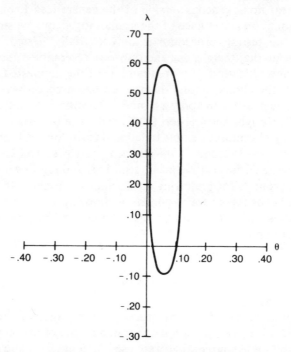

Source: Halvorsen and Pollakowski, "Choice of Functional Form for Hedonic Price Equations," p. 46.

Figure A–1. Ninety-nine Percent Confidence Region for θ and λ

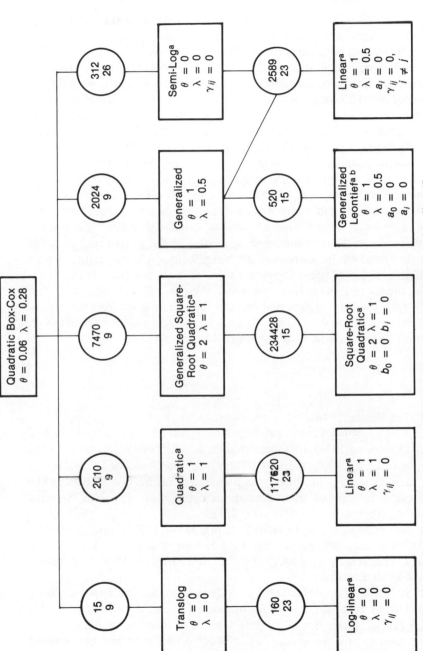

Source: Halvorsen and Pollakowski, "Choice of Functional Form for Hedonic Price Equations," p. 47.
Note: The top number in each circle is the value of the test statistic and the bottom number is the critical value at the .01 level.
[a]The form is rejected at the .01 level.
[b]Linear homogeneity imposed.

Figure A–2. Tests of Hypotheses

of the log likelihood was substantially more sensitive to the value of the transformation parameter for the dependent variable than to the value of the transformation parameter for the independent variables.

The translog, quadratic, generalized square-root quadratic, and non-homogeneous version of the generalized Leontief forms involve only the imposition of restrictions on the values of θ and λ. The values of (θ, λ) for each form are: translog (0.0, 0.0), quadratic (1.0, 1.0), generalized square-root quadratic (2.0, 1.0), and nonhomogeneous version of the generalized Leontief form (1.0, 0.5). As shown in figure A–1, the values of θ and λ corresponding to each of these forms lie outside the 99 percent confidence interval, and all these forms are accordingly rejected at the .01 level.

The test statistics and critical χ^2 values for each of the tests of hypotheses are shown in figure A–2. Since all other forms except the semi-log are conditional on the rejected translog, quadratic, generalized square-root quadratic, and nonhomogeneous version of the generalized Leontief forms, they need not be tested further. Nevertheless, it is interesting to note from figure A–2 that these forms are rejected even conditional on acceptance of the more general forms of which they are special cases.

The semi-log form is obtained from the quadratic Box-Cox form by imposing the restrictions $\theta = 0$, $\lambda = 1$, and $\gamma_{ij} = 0$. As shown in figure A–2, the semi-log form is also strongly rejected at the .01 level.[16]

Notes

1. See Rosen (1974).

2. The principal functional forms used have been linear (Kain and Quigley 1970; King 1973); log-linear (Kravis and Lipsey 1971); and semi-log (Griliches 1961; Kain and Quigley 1970; Ohta and Griliches 1975; Triplett 1969). In some cases, the functional form used has been modified by the limited use of interaction terms among the explanatory variables. See, for example, Grether and Mieszkowski (1974).

3. See Heckman and Polachek (1974), White (1972), and Zarembka (1968, 1974). Kau and Lee (1976*a*, 1976*b*) have examined the functional form of urban density gradients, and Kau and Sirmans (1979) have examined land value functions.

4. A flexible functional form provides a second-order approximation to an arbitrary twice-differentiable functional form; see Diewert (1974*a*) and Lau (1974). Examples of flexible forms are translog, quadratic, generalized square-root quadratic, square-root quadratic, and generalized Leontief.

5. See, for example, Atkinson and Halvorsen (1976); Berndt and Wood (1975); Christensen, Jorgenson, and Lau (1971,1973); Diewert (1971,

1974*a*, 1974*b*); Glandon and Pollakowski (1982*a*, 1982*b*); Halvorsen (1978); and Lau (1974).

6. A similar but somewhat more restrictive approach has been used in different contexts by Appelbaum (1979), Berndt and Khaled (1979), and Kiefer (1976). See, also, note 9 for this chapter.

7. The restrictions $\gamma_{ij} = \gamma_{ji}$ are imposed for purposes of identification only and place no effective constraints on the generality of the form. If the restrictions are not imposed, each coefficient γ_{ij} would be replaced by (γ_{ij} + γ_{ji})/2 and the γ_{ij} and γ_{ji} could not be separately identified.

8. A still more general functional form could be obtained by allowing $\lambda_i \neq \lambda_j$. Since all of the usual flexible functional forms impose the restriction $\lambda_i = \lambda_j = \lambda$, however, this generalization does not appear to be worth the considerable increase in computational cost that it would involve.

9. We know of no studies using a form similar to the quadratic Box-Cox for analyzing the choice of functional form for hedonic price equations. Kiefer (1976) uses a similar form to analyze the choice of functional form for indirect utility functions, but imposes the restriction $\theta = \lambda$. Berndt and Khaled (1979) use a similar form for cost functions, but impose the restriction $\theta = 2\lambda$. Appelbaum (1979) uses Box-Cox transformations of the explanatory variables in choosing between quadratic forms for production functions but does not transform the dependent variable.

10. The generalized square-root quadratic form is a generalization of the square-root quadratic form introduced by Diewert (1974*b*).

11. The restrictions $b_0 = b_i = 0$ imply that $\alpha_i = \Sigma_j\lambda_{ij}$ and $\Sigma_i\alpha_i = 1 + 2\alpha_0$. The square-root quadratic form is linear homogeneous.

12. The restrictions $a_0 = a_i = 0$ imply that $\alpha_i = 2 \Sigma_j\gamma_{ij}$ and $\Sigma_i\alpha_i = 1 + \alpha_0$.

13. This section is based on Box and Cox (1964).

14. The structural data are drawn from the BATSC Household Survey (1965). Census tract data are taken from the 1960 Census of Housing and the 1960 Census of Population. The employment accessibility index is the gravity index Σ_jE_j/d_j^2, where E_j is total employment in the jth census tract, d_j is free-flow driving time from the census tract in question to the jth census tract, and the summation is done over all census tracts except the one in question. The employment data are obtained from the BATSC Employment Inventory (1964); driving times are obtained from the Bay Area Simulation Study (1968).

15. The parameter estimates and their standard errors are available on request.

16. If a specific functional form were accepted, the resulting estimators would be preliminary test estimators with unknown statistical properties, and the usual hypothesis tests would not be valid. See Judge and Bock (1978).

Appendix B:
The Employment
Accessibility Index:
Data and Index Values

This appendix describes the data employed to construct the employment accessibility index defined and used in chapters 2 and 6. The number of existing jobs in each census tract was obtained from an additional BATSC file which contains an inventory of essentially all employment by Standard Industrial Classification (SIC) code and by zone. Given the definition of the zones, it was a relatively straightforward process to compute the total employment in each census tract in the Bay Area. The driving times between census tracts were obtained from the Bay Area Simulation Study (BASS). In this study, the nine-county Bay Area is divided into 617 BASS tracts, and driving times are estimated between all pairings of these tracts. These data were very useful for constructing an accessibility index at the census tract level, since the BASS tracts are usually coterminous with census tracts. In those cases where census tracts were aggregated to form a BASS tract, the same value of the driving time variable was assigned to each of the census tracts making up the BASS tract. In those cases where census tracts were split into more than one BASS tract, a simple mean of the driving times for the BASS tracts was employed. Since the nine-county Bay Area contains 742 census tracts, the former situation applied more frequently than the latter.

The driving times between two BASS tracts were computed by BASS as the free-flow driving time between BASS tract centroids. This driving time is calculated by employing airline distance as a basis and adjusting for geographical or topographical barriers and the resulting patterns of the system of streets. After the proportions of total trip length on local arterials and freeways were estimated, these distances were converted to times by using driving speeds derived from BATSC. These BATSC driving speeds were obtained by the BATSC staff by running actual driving tests on different types of roads in different parts of the Bay Area.

A more detailed description of the procedure employed to assign a travel time to a given trip between two BASS tracts is as follows. First, BASS tract centroids are assigned $x - y$ coordinates. This permits the linear distance between centroids to be calculated by use of the Pythagorean theorem. Next, the zones of origin and destination are determined. The nine-county Bay Area is divided into twenty-one zones for this purpose. The pair of zones involved determines the basic route of the trip—that is, the use of freeways, other roads, and so forth—and the freeway and nonfreeway speeds. Given the route, the characteristics of the trip with respect to terrain and water barriers and the general orientation of the road networks may be determined.

Where there are no physical barriers, the following procedure is employed. First, the distances of the origin and destination from the freeways used in the trip (if relevant) are estimated. The freeway distance traveled is then calculated by subtracting these nonfreeway distances from the total distance. The travel times on these segments are then calculated employing average freeway and nonfreeway speeds obtained from the BATSC, *Procedure Manual for Speed-Volume Runs* (1966). Total trip time is simply the summation of the travel times for each of the segments.

If there is a physical barrier, however, one of thirty-eight special routes (usually water routes via bridges) is assigned. The foregoing procedure is then employed to obtain travel times from the origin to the beginning of the special route and from the end of the special route to the destination. The travel time over the special route is then added to these travel times.

In order to reflect the time necessary to initiate a journey, a two-minute penalty is added to every trip. In addition, an efficiency factor is used for longer trips. It should also be noted that the BASS time-distance matrix is symmetric. Although travel times were different for different directions of travel (especially for the thirty-eight special routes), the BASS staff did not think that the additional accuracy to be obtained by considering these differences was worth the cost involved.

See Center for Real Estate and Urban Economics, *Jobs, People, and Land: Bay Area Simulation Study* (Berkeley, 1968), Appendix IV, for additional information about construction of the BASS time-distance matrix.

The values of the employment accessibility index that were constructed from these employment data and the distance-time matrix for the census tracts used in chapter 2 are shown in table B-1.

Table B-1
Values of the Employment Accessibility Variable
(JOBACC) for Census Tracts Used in Chapter 2

Census Tract	JOBACC
Albany	
AB 1	1.597
AB 2	1.597
AB 3	1.628
AB 4	1.628
AB 5	1.628

Table B-1 continued

Census Tract	JOBACC
Fremont	
FR 70	0.340
FR 71	0.340
FR 72	0.515
FR 73	0.575
FR 74	0.575
FR 75	0.628
Piedmont	
PI 7	1.643
PI 8	2.057
El Cerrito	
EC 84	1.479
EC 85	1.243
EC 86	1.479
EC 87	1.479
EC 88	1.644
EC 89	1.644
EC 90	1.424
San Pablo	
SP 64	0.544
SP 66	0.779
SP 68	1.061
SP 69	1.163
Mill Valley	
G 26	0.872
G 27	0.619
G 28	0.591
San Anselmo	
E 15	0.449
E 16	0.568
E 17	0.723
Belmont	
53	0.724
58	1.063
59	1.072
60	0.609
Burlingame	
33	1.463
34	1.463
35	1.359
36	1.268
37	1.268
38	1.317
Daly City	
11	2.328
12	2.355
13	2.068
14	1.452
16	2.108

Table B-1 continued

Census Tract	JOBACC
17	1.914
18	1.563
19	1.227
Menlo Park	
85	1.084
86	0.883
87	1.063
90	1.302
91	1.299
92	1.007
93	0.913
94	0.707
Millbrae	
29	1.351
30	1.189
31	1.197
32	1.074
Pacifica	
20	0.984
21	0.544
22	0.382
Redwood City	
66	1.111
67	1.107
68	0.949
69	0.718
71	0.698
72	0.716
74	1.114
75	1.114
76	1.315
77	1.058
80	0.822
San Bruno	
24	2.132
25	2.132
26	1.143
27	1.006
28	1.624
Campbell	
A 26	1.067
I 64	1.384
I 65	1.031
I 66	0.811
I 67	0.773
Los Altos	
N 100	0.997
N 101	0.766
N 102	1.068
N 103	1.068

Table B-1 continued

Census Tract	JOBACC
N 104	1.438
N 105	1.438
Mountain View	
M 91	1.397
N 92	1.321
N 93	1.391
N 94	1.431
N 95	1.642
N 96	1.642
N 97	1.642
N 98	1.394
N 99	1.203
Saratoga	
K 73	0.451
K 74	0.649
K 75	0.498
K 76	0.395

Appendix C: Construction of the Educational Expenditure per Pupil Variable Used in Chapter 2

It was necessary to construct the variable for current public educational expenditure per pupil for two reasons. First, since education cost is greater at higher grade levels, a weighted average of enrollments had to be employed. The following weights were considered most appropriate: kindergarten pupils, 0.6; elementary pupils (grades 1-8), 1.0; secondary school pupils (grades 9-12), 1.3; special pupils, 2. These were arrived at by examining Bay Area educational expenditures at different grade levels and are similar to those used by Kiesling (1967) for a sample of school districts in the state of New York.

Second, the data on expenditure and enrollment are available not by city but by elementary and secondary school districts. Typically, a city contains one or more elementary school districts, while high school districts usually coincide with a number of elementary districts. Since high school districts often contain portions of more than one city, adjustments had to be made in order to obtain per-pupil expenditure by city. The procedure adopted here was to impute the enrollment and expenditures of a high school district to the various elementary school districts that coincide with it. Once this was done, it was possible to obtain per-pupil expenditure P for any given city as follows:

$$P = \frac{a + b}{0.6_{E_k} + 1.0_{E_e} + 1.3(E_h + E_{ah}) + 2.0(E_{se} + E_{sh})}$$

where a is the current annual expenditure in relevant elementary school districts, and b is the estimated annual current high school expenditure on pupils residing within the city, which can be written as

$$f(ra_e + cra_e)/ah$$

where r is the county ratio of high school enrollment to elementary enrollment, c is adult average daily attendance (a.d.a.) in relevant high school district divided by nonadult a.d.a. in relevant high school district, a_e is elementary pupil a.d.a., a_h is a.d.a. in relevant high school, and f is the annual current expenditure in relevant high school district; and where E_k is kindergarten enrollment, E_e is elementary enrollment, $E_h = a(E_k + E_e)$, $E_{ah} = cE_h$, E_{se} is elementary special pupil enrollment, and $E_{sh} = (E_h/d)n$, where d is enrollment in relevant secondary school, and n is the number of special pupils in relevant high school district.

The data employed in constructing this variable are listed in table 2–4 in chapter 2.

Appendix D: Distribution of Owner-Occupied Single-Family Dwelling Units, by Number of Rooms by Census Tract (for Data Used in Chapter 2)

Table D-1

| | Number of Rooms | | | | |
Census Tract	4 or Fewer	5	6	7	8 or More
Albany					
AB 1	0	4	7	1	0
AB 2	1	6	3	0	0
AB 3	2	5	5	1	0
AB 4	0	2	2	1	0
AB 5	1	4	1	1	0
Fremont					
FR 70	1	9	9	3	2
FR 71	1	4	17	18	15
FR 72	1	31	45	21	7
FR 73	0	26	44	26	14
FR 74	3	17	10	6	0
FR 75	1	7	5	5	0
Piedmont					
PI 7	0	0	4	1	26
PI 8	2	4	4	11	14
El Cerrito					
EC 84	1	4	9	7	9
EC 85	1	3	10	3	3
EC 86	1	3	5	3	0
EC 87	2	3	1	1	2
EC 88	1	8	8	1	0
EC 89	0	5	4	3	0
EC 90	3	10	10	5	8
San Pablo					
SP 64	0	1	0	0	0
SP 66	5	12	8	6	0
SP 68	2	8	6	1	0
SP 69	0	3	2	2	1
Mill Valley					
G 26	2	16	1?	7	13
G 27	6	7	7	7	9
G 28	0	0	1	0	0

Table D–1 continued

Census Tract	Number of Rooms				
	4 or Fewer	5	6	7	8 or More
San Anselmo					
E 15	5	15	6	4	5
E 16	2	3	3	4	0
E 17	3	5	5	1	3
Belmont					
53	0	1	1	0	0
58	0	3	4	3	1
59	2	8	6	5	3
60	3	14	14	8	3
Burlingame					
33	0	5	3	0	0
34	3	5	2	2	4
35	0	2	3	1	4
36	1	3	8	1	6
37	1	3	4	1	7
38	1	5	4	10	5
Daly City					
11	1	12	0	1	0
12	2	7	8	3	0
13	0	10	10	1	1
14	0	10	10	2	1
16	1	11	12	1	1
17	3	2	2	0	0
18	0	7	30	8	0
19	1	9	14	1	1
Menlo Park					
85	0	2	2	1	0
86	1	1	2	0	0
87	0	3	2	0	2
90	2	5	12	4	2
91	1	4	0	1	2
92	0	3	2	3	2
93	0	3	7	2	0
94	0	2	2	1	5
Millbrae					
29	0	3	1	1	0
30	0	6	21	9	5
31	1	2	6	4	2
32	0	1	3	4	3
Pacifica					
20	2	12	20	3	1
21	3	11	12	5	1
22	0	9	41	4	4
Redwood City					
66	0	2	0	0	0
67	1	1	7	2	2
68	0	4	4	5	4
69	4	3	3	1	1
71	0	9	14	5	3

Table D-1 continued

Census Tract	Number of Rooms				
	4 or Fewer	5	6	7	8 or More
Redwood City					
72	0	8	6	2	0
74	4	4	0	0	0
75	1	2	3	0	0
76	0	0	1	0	0
77	1	0	4	0	1
80	0	1	0	0	0
San Bruno					
24	1	8	4	1	0
25	0	5	1	0	0
26	0	26	17	6	4
27	1	9	15	11	2
28	5	16	15	5	2
Campbell					
A 26	0	3	4	1	0
I 64	0	0	2	1	0
I 65	2	8	3	0	1
I 66	0	5	8	3	1
I 67	0	4	7	2	2
Los Altos					
N 100	0	2	12	12	4
N 101	1	1	2	3	5
N 102	1	8	12	5	5
N 103	2	7	5	4	1
N 104	0	3	2	7	2
N 105	2	5	7	3	7
Mountain View					
M 91	2	1	0	1	0
M 92	3	2	6	4	1
N 93	1	6	4	3	0
N 94	1	0	0	0	0
N 95	1	1	5	1	0
N 96	0	4	1	1	0
N 97	0	2	2	1	0
N 98	0	15	12	3	1
N 99	0	3	4	4	5
Saratoga					
K 73	2	1	5	7	12
K 74	0	7	17	10	4
K 75	1	2	1	9	13
K 76	1	3	6	4	2

Appendix E: Available Combinations of Dwelling Unit Attributes, Owner-Occupied Single-Family Dwelling Units (for Data Used in Chapter 2)

Table E-1

Census Tract	Number of Dwelling Unit Size, Lot Size Combinations	Number of Dwelling Unit Size, Age Combinations	Number of Observations
Albany			
AB 1	4	3	12
AB 2	3	2	10
AB 3	4	2	13
AB 4	3	3	5
AB 5	4	3	7
Fremont			
FR 70	6	5	24
FR 71	8	6	55
FR 72	7	6	105
FR 73	8	5	110
FR 74	5	4	36
FR 75	4	4	18
Piedmont			
PI 7	4	4	31
PI 8	7	4	35
El Cerrito			
EC 84	7	6	30
EC 85	6	5	20
EC 86	4	4	12
EC 87	5	4	9
EC 88	3	3	18
EC 89	4	4	12
EC 90	7	6	36
San Pablo			
SP 64	1	1	1
SP 66	6	4	31
SP 68	4	4	17
SP 69	4	5	8
Mill Valley			
G 26	7	6	50
G 27	7	6	36
G 28	1	1	1

Table E-1 continued

Census Tract	Number of Dwelling Unit Size, Lot Size Combinations	Number of Dwelling Unit Size, Age Combinations	Number of Observations
San Anselmo			
E 15	6	6	35
E 16	5	2	12
E 17	9	6	17
Belmont			
53	2	2	2
58	4	4	11
59	7	6	24
60	6	4	42
Burlingame			
33	2	2	8
34	6	3	16
35	3	3	10
36	6	3	19
37	6	4	16
38	7	5	25
Daly City			
11	3	3	14
12	4	3	20
13	6	5	22
14	5	5	23
16	5	5	26
17	3	4	7
18	4	3	45
19	5	4	26
Menlo Park			
85	3	4	5
86	3	2	4
87	3	5	7
90	6	5	25
91	5	3	8
92	4	6	10
93	4	3	12
94	4	4	10
Millbrae			
29	2	4	5
30	6	6	41
31	3	5	15
32	5	3	11
Pacifica			
20	7	5	38
21	6	5	32
22	6	4	58
Redwood City			
66	1	2	2
67	4	4	13
68	6	5	17
69	6	5	12

Table E-1 continued

Census Tract	Number of Dwelling Unit Size, Lot Size Combinations	Number of Dwelling Unit Size, Age Combinations	Number of Observations
71	7	5	31
72	4	3	16
74	3	2	8
75	2	3	6
76	1	1	1
77	3	3	6
80	1	1	1
San Bruno			
24	4	4	14
25	3	2	6
26	6	3	53
27	6	3	38
28	6	5	43
Campbell			
A 26	2	3	8
I 64	1	1	3
I 65	5	5	14
I 66	4	3	17
I 67	4	5	15
Los Altos			
N 100	5	4	30
N 101	6	3	11
N 102	6	6	31
N 103	6	5	19
N 104	6	5	14
N 105	6	6	24
Mountain View			
M 91	3	3	4
N 92	5	5	16
N 93	4	3	14
N 94	1	1	1
N 95	3	2	8
N 96	2	2	6
N 97	3	3	5
N 98	6	4	31
N 99	7	5	16
Saratoga			
K 73	6	6	27
K 74	5	4	38
K 75	6	3	26
K 76	5	5	16

Note: See text for an explanation of the construction of this table.

Appendix F:
Simple Correlations among Dwelling Unit Attributes, Owner-Occupied Single-Family Dwelling Units (for Data Used in Chapter 2)

	NROOMS	AGEDUM1	AGEDUM2	AGEDUM3	LOTSIZ	MEDRMS	DENSITY
NROOMS	1.000						
AGEDUM1	0.088	1.000					
AGEDUM2	−0.140	−0.217	1.000				
AGEDUM3	−0.093	−0.429	−0.375	1.000			
LOTSIZ	0.256	0.141	−0.061	−0.038	1.000		
MEDRMS	0.348	−0.019	−0.160	0.093	0.148	1.000	
DENSITY	−0.161	−0.198	−0.026	0.033	−0.093	−0.378	1.000
GOLF	0.077	0.049	0.017	−0.072	−0.023	0.046	−0.029
MOUNTS	0.118	0.048	−0.053	0.017	0.138	0.217	−0.134
CRIME	−0.141	−0.114	−0.082	0.033	−0.202	−0.300	0.321
JOBACC	−0.019	0.268	0.173	−0.097	−0.212	−0.038	−0.295
EDUEXP	0.032	0.191	0.153	−0.010	−0.005	0.033	−0.441
FIRE	−0.051	0.145	0.097	0.006	−0.113	−0.014	−0.352
PARKEX	0.125	0.252	0.068	−0.131	−0.017	0.023	−0.016
TAXRT	0.104	0.120	−0.006	−0.051	0.072	0.126	0.084

GOLF	MOUNTS	CRIME	JOBACC	EDUEXP	FIRE	PARKEX	TAXRT
1.000							
0.333	1.000						
−0.074	−0.178	1.000					
0.171	−0.183	−0.077	1.000				
0.138	0.124	−0.282	0.460	1.000			
0.012	−0.020	−0.048	0.619	0.378	1.000		
0.259	0.097	−0.142	0.231	0.194	−0.095	1.000	
0.075	0.105	−0.301	−0.003	−0.263	−0.039	0.451	1.000

Appendix G:
The Multinomial
Logit Model

McFadden (1974a) outlines a general procedure for formulating econometric models of population choice behavior in cases where alternatives are qualitative and develops a specific multinomial logit model that is empirically estimable. Drawing on the work of Luce (1959) and others, he discusses the underlying axioms that give rise to this model. He also describes the empirical estimation of the model and the statistical properties of the results obtained by employing it. Additional discussion of the multinomial logit model and applications of it are found in McFadden (1975, 1976a), dealing with urban freeway routing, and in McFadden (1974b) and Domencich and McFadden (1975), dealing with urban travel demand. Further applications include Boskin's (1974) work on occupational choice, Radner and Miller's (1970) and Kohn, Manski and Mundel's (1976) work on choice of college, and Miller and Lerman's (1979, 1981) work on retail location. McFadden (1976b) presents a survey of the historical development of models of this sort as well as a survey of empirical applications. McFadden (1978) also discusses issues involved in modeling the choice of residential location. Recent econometric advances by Manski and Lerman (1977), Manski and McFadden (1981), Lerman and Manski (1979), and Cosslett (1978) have made it possible to estimate such models from a greater range of possible data sets. Finally, research by Koppelman (1975), Lerman and Manski (1981), McFadden and Reid (1975), and others has provided a rich array of possible techniques for making aggregate-level forecasts using models estimated at the disaggregate, or micro, level. The following is a summary of McFadden's (1974a) development of the multinomial logit model.

An individual in the population is assumed to have a set of measured attributes sCS, where S is the set of all possible and relevant measured attributes, and s is the vector of values of those attributes possessed by this individual. This individual faces a set of J alternatives indexed by $J = 1,2, \ldots ,$ J, and described by attributes x_j. The individual is assumed to select the alternative, x_j, that maximizes his utility.

Suppose his utility function can be written

$$u = V(s,x) + \epsilon(s,x) \tag{G.1}$$

where V is nonstochastic and reflects the representative tastes of the population, and ϵ is stochastic and reflects random variation in the utility func-

121

tions of individuals with characteristics s facing alternatives with attributes x. Each individual confronts a fixed set of alternatives B, which is a subset of the full range of alternatives. Given that individuals choose the alternative, x_i, that maximizes their utility, we can express the probability that an individual drawn randomly from the population with characteristics s and alternative set B will select x_i as

$$P_i = P(x_i|s,B) \tag{G.2}$$

$$= P(V(s,x_i) + \epsilon(s,x_i) > V(s,x_j) + \epsilon(s,x_j) \text{ for all } j \neq i)$$

$$= P(V_i - V_j + \epsilon_i > \epsilon_j \text{ for all } j \neq i)$$

where $V_i = V(s,x_i)$ and $\epsilon_i = \epsilon_i(s,x_i)$.

Certain specifications of the joint distributions of the ϵ_j should allow the computation of econometrically useful formulas for the P_i. McFadden notes that these specifications are difficult to define in practice. Instead, he specifies a set of restrictions on the selection probabilities (P_i) and considers whether those restrictions are consistent with some distribution of utility maximizing individuals.

McFadden then identifies three restrictions on the selection probabilities, which, when combined with the assumption that the stochastic distribution of utility maximizing individuals is Weibull (Gnedenlso, extreme value), allow him to derive the multinomial logit model. The three restrictions on selection probabilities are: (1) independence of irrelevant alternatives, (2) positivity, and (3) irrelevance of alternative set effect.

The independence of irrelevant alternatives restriction requires that, for all possible alternative sets B, measured attributes s, and members x and y of B:

$$P(x|s,\{x,y\})P(y|s,B) = P(y|s,\{x,y\}) P(x|s,B) \tag{G.3}$$

If $P(x|s,B)$ is positive, then this implies that $P(x|s,\{x,y\})$ is also positive, and

$$\frac{P(y|s,\{x,y\})}{P(x|s,\{x,y\})} = \frac{P(y|s,B)}{P(x|s,B)} \tag{G.4}$$

that is, the relative odds of a choice of y over x are identical if it is a simple binary choice or if it is a multinomial choice over the choice set B.

The positivity restriction requires that $P(x|s,B) > 0$ for all possible alternative sets B, vectors of measured attributes s, and $x \in B$. This is a technical requirement to avoid analytic difficulties that would prevent the simple derivation of equation G.4 from equation G.3.

Suppose that B consists of the set $\{x,y,z\}$. Let $P_{xy} = P(x|s,\{x,y\})$. Then, from equation G.4 we obtain

$$P(y|s,B) = \frac{P_{yx}}{P_{xy}} P(x|s,B) \qquad (G.5)$$

so that

$$1 = \sum_{y \in B} P(y|s,B) = \left(\sum_{y \in B} \frac{P_{yx}}{P_{xy}} \right) P(x|s,B) \qquad (G.6)$$

and

$$P(x|s,B) = \frac{1}{\left(\sum_{y \in B} P_{yx}/P_{xy} \right)} \qquad (G.7)$$

From equation G.5, letting $P(y|s,B) = P_y$, we have

$$\frac{P_y}{P_z} = \frac{P_{yz}}{P_{zy}}$$

$$\frac{P_x}{P_z} = \frac{P_{xz}}{P_{zx}}$$

Therefore,

$$\frac{P_{yx}}{P_{xy}} = \frac{P_{yz}/P_{zy}}{P_{xz}/P_{zx}} \qquad (G.8)$$

Let $V(s,x,z) = \log(P_{xz}/P_{zx})$. Then, if z is taken as a benchmark member of B, from equations G.7 and G.8, we have

$$P(x|s,B) = \frac{e^{V(s,x,z)}}{\sum_{y \in B} e^{V(s,y,z)}} \qquad (G.9)$$

McFadden notes that, in $V(s,x,z)$, which is the individual's hypothesized utility function, s may be thought of as the "measured taste effect," x as the "choice alternative effect," and z as the "alternative set effect." (McFadden 1974a, p. 110).

The irrelevance of alternative set effect restriction requires that the function $V(s,x,z)$ be additively separable. This is an identifying restriction employed to isolate the choice alternative effect when the alternative set effect cannot be identified. Given this restriction, equation G9 may be rewritten as

$$P(x|s,B) = \frac{e^{v(s,x)}}{\sum\limits_{y \in B} e^{v(s,y)}} \qquad (G.10)$$

Assume that the function $v(x,s)$ is linear in parameters. We can then write the relative odds of choosing location i over location j as

$$\log(P_i|P_j) = \sum_{k=1}^{K} \beta_k (z_k^i - z_k^j) \qquad (G.11)$$

is the kth attribute of the ith alternative. The elasticity of demand for the ith alternative with respect to the kth attribute of the ith alternative, then, is

$$\beta_k z_k^i (1 - P_i) \qquad (G.12)$$

where

$$P_i = \frac{e^{\beta'z^i}}{\sum\limits_{j=1}^{J} e^{\beta'z^j}}$$

The cross elasticity of demand for the ith alternative with respect to the kth attribute of the jth alternative is

$$-\beta_k z_k^j P_j \qquad (G.13)$$

(Domenrich and McFadden 1975, pp. 83–85).

The parameter β_k can be estimated by maximizing the appropriate log likelihood function employing an iterative procedure (McFadden 1974a, pp. 113–115).

Three features of the multinomial logit model deserve further comment. First, the model assumes that each individual's utility function has two components: systematic and stochastic. This distinguishes the multinomial logit model from deterministic statistical models of consumer choice, which recognize only the systematic character of individual choices. In the deterministic models, any nonsystematic variation in consumption choices is ascribed either to a misspecification of the model or to measurement errors. While the deterministic models are generally plausible when the objects of choice can be varied continuously (for example, the quantity of sugar), a model that allows behavioral determinants of individual choices to have both systematic and random elements may be more plausible when those choices are discrete. The grounds for this assertion are that discrete choices, even given perfect information, may force the individual to choose between two or more alternatives having substantially different characteristics when the individual is indifferent, or nearly indifferent, between them. Measurement error would not adequately explain a choice made under these circumstances, while random variations in individual utility functions would be consistent with such choices. Although the multinomial logit model is not the only statistical model that allows stochastic elements in individual utility functions (the probit model is another example of such a model), it is a useful model that does so.

Second, the multinomial logit model allows the choices that an individual makes to depend on both the characteristics of the chooser and the characteristics of the alternatives. Important interactions between choice characteristics and chooser characteristics can thus be readily incorporated into the model.

Third, the multinomial logit model requires a strong assumption, known as independence of irrelevant alternatives. Independence of irrelevant alternatives requires that altering the set of alternatives not affect the relative odds of choosing between any two alternatives. This assumption is implausible whenever some of the feasible alternatives are perceived by the chooser as very similar. McFadden provides an instructive example of this. Suppose, he suggests, that a boy can choose between a green bike and a horse. Next, suppose we offer him a third alternative, a blue bike. It is reasonable to assume that the probability of his choosing the horse will be altered only slightly, if at all, by provision of this third alternative. The probability of his choosing the green bike, however, is likely to drop substantially. In short, we would expect in this case that the relative odds of his selecting the green bike over the horse will decline when we add the blue bike as a third alternative. The multinomial logit model's independence of irrelevant alternatives assumption is inconsistent with these expectations, since it requires that the relative odds of the boy selecting the green bike over the horse remain unchanged when we add the blue bike as an alternative.

Nested multinomial logit models provide one means of making the independence of irrelevant alternatives assumption more plausible. A nested model describes the choice process as if it were sequential, with the more general choices (such as between a horse and a bike) being made in one step and more specific choices within a general choice (such as a blue or a green bike) being made in subsequent steps. It is reasonable to assume that adding a yellow bike to the second-stage choice would satisfy the independence of irrelevant alternatives' assumption for that choice. This does not entirely circumvent the implausibility of the independence of irrelevant alternatives assumption, since that assumption requires that altering the set of alternatives in the second stage not alter the first-stage choice probabilities. If choosers are utility maximizers, this implies that first-stage choices are made only with full knowledge of the optimal second-stage choices. Nevertheless, if the first-stage choices can be categorized such that alternatives within each category are homogeneous, the independence of irrelevant alternatives assumption will be fairly plausible.

Weisbrod (1978) provides an example of a nested multinomial logit model by considering (1) the joint choice of whether or not to move and the tenure type chosen; (2) for movers, the joint choice of residential location, housing type, and automobile ownership; and (3) the choice of mode to work and destination for shopping trips. Moving decisions depend in part on the estimated utility of current and alternative locations, and location and automobile ownership decisions depend in part on estimates of the travel accessibility for every alternative choice.

It is worth noting that the multinomial logit model permits one to test the plausibility of a nested, as opposed to a simultaneous, model. A nested model aggregates alternatives that are presumed to be viewed as similar by the chooser. To the extent that this presumption is correct, the nested model, which provides estimates of the probability of selecting a particular *type* of alternative (e.g., an owner-occupied house vs. a rental unit) is sensible. If, however, all alternatives are viewed as dissimilar, a simultaneous model is correct. The multinomial logit model allows one to estimate a coefficient that measures the degree of perceived similarity of alternatives. (This is the coefficient on the log of the number of alternatives in each category. See McFadden (1978)). As this coefficient approaches zero, it indicates that alternatives within each category are viewed as similar; hence, the nested model applies. As this coefficient approaches unity, it indicates that alternatives within each class are viewed as dissimilar, and the simultaneous model applies. If the coefficient falls outside these bounds, the independence of irrelevant alternatives assumption and the assumption of a utility-maximizing choice calculus are violated.

In sum, the multinomial logit model provides a plausible and tractable statistical model of discrete choice. By assuming that utility functions have both systematic and stochastic elements, it provides a more plausible model of discrete choice than deterministic statistical models do. By allowing choices to depend on characteristics of the chooser as well as of the alternatives, it incorporates important interactions between these two types of characteristics. Its assumption of the independence of irrelevant alternatives, however, undermines its plausibility for many analyses. Nested logit models partially circumvent this weakness, and their reasonableness is testable within the framework of the logit model.

Bibliography

Aaron, H. 1970. "Income Taxes and Housing." *American Economic Review* 60 (December):789–806.

Alonso, W. 1964. *Location and Land Use*. Cambridge, Mass.: Harvard University Press.

Appelbaum, E. 1979. "On the Choice of Functional Form." *International Economic Review* 20 (June):449–458.

Atkinson, S.E., and Halvorsen, R. 1976. "Interfuel Substitution in Steam Electric Power Generation." *Journal of Political Economy* 84: 959–978.

Berndt, E.; Darrough, M.; and Diewert, W. 1977. "Flexible Functional Forms and Expenditure Distributions: An Application to Canadian Consumer Demand Functions." *International Economic Review* 18: 651–675.

Berndt, E., and Khaled, M. 1979. "Parametric Productivity Measurement and Choice Among Flexible Functional Forms." *Journal of Political Economy* 87 (December):1220–1245.

Berndt, E., and Wood, D. 1975. "Technology, Prices, and the Derived Demand for Energy." *Review of Economics and Statistics* 57:259–268.

Bloom, H.S.; Ladd, H.F.; and Yinger, J. *Intrajurisdictional Property Tax Capitalization*. New York: Academic Press, forthcoming.

Boskin, M.J. 1974. "A Conditional Logit Model of Occupational Choice." *Journal of Political Economy* 82 (March-April):389–398.

Box, G.E.P., and Cox, D.R. 1964. "An Analysis of Transformations." *Journal of the Royal Statistical Society (B)* 26:211–252.

Brown, G.M., Jr., and Pollakowski, H.O. 1977. "Economic Valuation of Shoreline." *Review of Economics and Statistics* 59 (August):272–278.

Brown, G.M., Jr., and Pollakowski, H.O. 1979. "Economic Valuation of Shoreline: A Reply." *Review of Economics and Statistics* 62 (November):635–636.

Case, K.E. 1978. *Property Taxation: The Need for Reform*. Cambridge, Mass.: Ballinger.

Castle, E.N.; Singh, A.; and Brown, W. 1964. *An Economic Evaluation of the Oregon Salmon and Steelhead Sport Fishery*. Technical Bulletin No. 78, Oregon State University Agricultural Experiment Station, Corvallis.

Christensen, L.; Jorgenson, D.; and Lau, L. 1971. "Conjugate Duality and the Transcendental Logarithmic Production Function." *Econometrica* 39:255–256.

Christensen, L.; Jorgenson, D.; and Lau, L. 1973. "Transcendental Logarithmic Production Frontiers." *Review of Economics and Statistics* 55:28–45.

Cosslett, S.R. 1978. "Efficient Estimation of Discrete Choice Models from Enriched Samples." Paper presented at Conference on Decision Risks and Uncertainty, Carnegie-Mellon University, 30 March–1 April.

Davis, R.K. 1964. "The Value of Big Game Hunting in a Private Forest." In *Transactions of the Twenty-ninth North American Wildlife and Natural Resources Conference,* pp. 393–403. Washington, D.C.: Wildlife Management Institute.

Diamond, D.B. 1975. "Income and Residence Location in Urban Areas." Working paper, Department of Economics, University of Chicago (December).

Diewert, W. 1971. "An Application of the Shepard Duality Theorem: A Generalized Leontief Production Function." *Journal of Political Economy* 79:481–507.

———. 1974*a.* "Applications of Duality Theory." In *Frontiers of Quantitative Economics,* ed. M. Intriligator and D. Kendrick, pp. 106–171. Amsterdam: North-Holland.

———. 1974*b.* "Functional Forms for Revenue and Factor Requirements Functions." *International Economic Review* 15:119–130.

Domencich, F., and McFadden, D. 1975. *"Urban Travel Demand: A Behavioral Analysis."* Charles Rivers Associates, Inc., Research Monograph. Amsterdam: North Holland.

Dornbusch, D.M., and Barrager, S.M. 1972. *Benefit of Water Pollution Control on Property Values.* Washington, D.C.: U.S. Environmental Protection Agency.

Edel, M., and Sclar, E. 1974. "Taxes, Spending, and Property Values: Supply Adjustment in a Tiebout-Oates Model." *Journal of Political Economy* 82 (September-October):941–954.

Ellickson, B. 1981. "An Alternative Test of the Hedonic Theory of Housing Markets." *Journal of Urban Economics* 9 (January): 56–79.

Epple, D., and Zelenitz, A. 1981. "The Roles of Jurisdictional Competition and of Collective Choice Institutions in the Market for Local Public Goods." *American Economic Review* 71 (May):87–91.

Epple, D.; Zelenitz, A.; and Visscher, M. 1978. "A Search for Testable Implications of the Tiebout Hypothesis." *Journal of Political Economy* 86 (June):405–425.

Fisher, F.M. 1970. "Tests of Equality Between Sets of Coefficients in Two Linear Regressions: An Expository Note." *Econometrica* 38 (March): 361–366.

Freeman, A.M. 1974. "On Estimating Air Pollution Control Benefits from Land Value Studies." *Journal of Environmental Economics and Management* 1 (May):74–83.

————. 1979. "Economic Valuation of Shoreline: A Comment." *Review of Economics and Statistics* 61 (November):634–635.

Friedman, J. 1975. "Household Location and the Supply of Local Public Services." Report No. P-5421, Rand Corporation, Santa Monica.

Glandon, G., and Pollakowski, H.O. 1982*a*. "Input Substitution in the Production of Housing Services." Working paper, MIT-Harvard Joint Center for Urban Studies.

Glandon, G., and Pollakowski, H.O. 1982*b*. "The Residential Demand for Energy." Working paper, MIT-Harvard Joint Center for Urban Studies.

Goldfeld, S.M., and Quandt, R.E. 1965. "Some Tests for Homoscedasticity." *Journal of the American Statistical Association* 60 (June): 539–547.

Goodman, A.C. 1978. "Hedonic Prices, Price Indices and Housing Markets." *Journal of Urban Economics* 5 (October): 471–484.

Grether, D.M., and Mieszkowski, P. 1974. "Determinants of Real Estate Values." *Journal of Urban Economics* 1 (April):127–146.

Griliches, Z. 1961. "Hedonic Price Indexes of Automobiles: An Econometric Analysis of Quality Change." The Price Statistics of the Federal Government, General Series No. 73. New York: National Bureau of Economic Research.

————. 1967. "Hedonic Price Indexes Revisited: Some Notes on the State of the Art." In American Statistical Association, *Proceedings of the Business and Economic Statistics Section,* pp. 324–332.

Halvorsen, R. 1978. *Econometric Models of U.S. Energy Demand.* Lexington, Mass.: Lexington Books, D.C. Heath.

Halvorsen, R., and Palmquist, R. 1980. "The Interpretation of Dummy Variables in Semi-Logarithmic Equations." *American Economic Review* 70 (September):474–475.

Halvorsen, R., and Pollakowski, H.O. 1981*a*. "Choice of Functional Form for Hedonic Price Equations." *Journal of Urban Economics* 10 (July): 37–49.

Halvorsen, R., and Pollakowski, H.O. 1981*b*. "The Effects of Fuel Prices on House Prices." *Urban Studies* 18 (June):205–211.

Hamilton, B. 1976. "The Effects of Property Taxes and Local Public Spending on Property Values: A Theoretical Comment." *Journal of Political Economy* 84 (June):647–650.

Hammack, J.M., and Brown, G.M. 1974. *Waterfowl and Wetlands: Toward Bio-economic Analysis.* Baltimore: Johns Hopkins Press.

Heckman, J., and Polachek, S. 1974. "Empirical Evidence on the Functional Form of the Earnings-schooling Relationship." *Journal of the American Statistical Association* 69: 350–354.

Ingram, G.K., ed. 1977. *Residential Location and Urban Housing Markets.* Cambridge, Mass.: Ballinger.

Ingram, G.K.; Kain, J.F.; and Ginn, J.R. 1972. *The Detroit Prototype of the NBER Urban Simulation Model.* New York: National Bureau of Economic Research.

Judge, G., and Bock, M. 1978. *The Statistical Implications of Pre-Test and Stein-Rule Estimators in Econometrics.* Amsterdam, North Holland.

Kain, J.K., and Quigley, J.M. 1970. "Measuring the Value of Housing Quality." *Journal of the American Statistical Association* 65 (June): 532–548.

Kau, J.B., and Lee, C.F. 1976*a*. "Functional Form, Density Gradient, and Price Elasticity of Demand for Housing." *Urban Studies* 13: 193–200.

Kau, J.B., and Lee, C.F. 1976*b*. "The Functional Form in Estimating the Density Gradient: An Empirical Investigation." *Journal of the American Statistical Association* 71:326–327.

Kau, J.B., and Sirmans, C.F. 1979. "Urban Land Value Functions and the Price Elasticity of Demand for Housing." *Journal of Urban Economics* 6:112–121.

Keifer, N. 1976. "Quadratic Utility Labor Supply and Commodity Demand. In *Studies in Non-linear Estimation,* ed. L. Goldfield and R. Quandt. Cambridge, Mass.: Ballinger.

Kiesling, J. 1967. "Measuring a Local Government Service: A Study of School Districts in New York State." *Review of Economics and Statistics* 49 (August):356–367.

King, A.T. 1973. *Property Taxes, Amenities, and Residential Land Values.* Cambridge: Ballinger.

———. 1974. "A Model of Residential Location Choice." Paper presented at the winter meetings of the Econometric Society, San Francisco, December.

———. 1975. "The Demand for Housing: Integrating the Roles of Journey-to-Work, Neighborhood Quality, and Prices." In *Household Production and Consumption,* ed. N.E. Terleckyj, pp. 451–483. New York: National Bureau of Economic Research.

———. 1976. "The Demand for Housing: A Lancastrian Approach," *Southern Economic Journal* 43:1077–1087.

———. 1977. Estimating Property Tax Capitalization: A Critical Comment." *Journal of Political Economy* 85 (April):425–431.

Kohn, M.G.; Manski, C.F.; and Mundell, D.S. 1976. "An Empirical Investigation of Factors which Influence College-Going Behavior." *Annals of Economic and Social Measurement* 5 (Fall):391–419.

Koppelman, F. 1975. "Travel Prediction with Models of Individual Choice Behavior." Ph.D. dissertation, Department of Civil Engineering, Massachusetts Institute of Technology.

Kravis, I., and Lipsey, R. 1971. *Price Competition in World Trade.* New York: National Bureau of Economic Research.

Krutilla, J.V., and Fisher, A.C. 1975. *The Economics of Natural Environments: Studies in the Valuation of Commodity and Amenity Resources.* Baltimore: Johns Hopkins Press.

Lancaster, Kelvin J. 1966. "A New Approach to Consumer Theory." *Journal of Political Economy* 74 (April):132–157.

———. 1971. *Consumer Demand: A New Approach.* New York: Columbia University Press.

Lau, L. 1974. "Applications of Duality Theory: a Comment." In *Frontiers of Quantitative Economics,* ed. M. Intriligator and D. Kendrick, pp. 176–199. North Holland.

Lerman, S.R. 1976. "Location, Housing, Automobile Ownership and Mode to Work: A Joint Choice Model." *Transportation Research Record,* no. 610, pp. 6–11.

———. 1979. "Neighborhood Choice and Transportation Services." In *The Economics of Neighborhood,* ed. D. Segal. New York: Academic Press.

Lerman, S.R., and Manski, C.F. 1979. "Sample Design for Discrete Choice Analysis of Travel Behavior: The State of the Art." *Transportation Research* 13a.

Lerman, S.R., and Manski, C.F. 1981. "On the Use of Simulated Frequencies to Approximate Choice Probabilities." In *Structural Analysis of Discrete Data: with Econometric Applications,* ed. C.F. Manski and D. McFadden. Cambridge, Mass.: MIT Press.

Lerman, S.R., Pollakowski, H.O., and Segal, D. 1981. "Employment Location, Demographic Change, and Inner City Revival." Paper presented at the winter meetings of the American Real Estate and Urban Economics Association, Washington, D.C., December.

Leven, C.L., and Mark, J.H. 1977. "A Revealed Preference Model for Analyzing Interneighbourhood Mobility." *Urban Studies* 14 (May): 147–160.

Linneman, P. 1980. "Some Empirical Results on the Nature of the Hedonic Price Function for the Urban Housing Market." *Journal of Urban Economics* 8 (July):47–68.

Luce, R. 1959. *Individual Choice Behavior.* New York: Wiley.

McFadden, D. 1974a. "Conditional Logit Analysis of Qualitative Choice Behavior." In *Frontiers in Econometrics,* ed. P. Zarembka. New York: Academic Press.

———. 1974b. "Measurement of Urban Travel Demand." *Journal of Public Economics* 3 (June):303–327.

———. 1975. "The Revealed Preferences of a Government Bureaucracy: Theory." *Bell Journal of Economics* 6 (Autumn):401–416.

———. 1976a. "The Revealed Preference of a Government Bureaucracy: Empirical Evidence." *Bell Journal of Economics* 7 (Spring):55–72.

————. 1976*b*. "Quantal Choice Analysis: A Survey." *Annals of Social and Economic Measurement* 5 (Fall):363–390.

————. 1978. "Modelling the Choice of Residential Location," *Transportation Research Record,* no. 673, pp. 72–77.

McFadden, D., and Reid, F. 1975. "Aggregate Travel Demand Forecasting from Disaggregated Behavioral Models." Mimeographed.

Manski, C.F., and Lerman, S.R. 1977. "The Estimation of Probabilities from Choice Based Samples." *Econometrica* 45:1977–1988.

Manski, C.F., and McFadden, D. 1981. "Alternative Estimators and Sample Designs for Discrete Choice Analysis." In *Structural Analysis of Discrete Data: with Econometric Applications,* ed. C.F. Manski and D. McFadden. Cambridge, Mass.: MIT Press.

Mathews, S.B., and Brown, G.M. 1970. *Economic Evaluation of the 1967 Sport Salmon Fisheries of Washington.* Technical Report No. 2. Olympia: Washington Department of Fisheries.

Mayo, S.K. 1975. "Local Public Goods and Residential Location: An Empirical Test of the Tiebout Hypothesis." In *Public Needs and Private Behavior in Metropolitan Areas,* ed. J.E. Jackson. Cambridge, Mass.: Ballinger.

Meador, M., and Pollakowski, H.O. 1981. "A Model of Property Tax Assessment Evaluation." Working paper, MIT-Harvard Joint Center for Urban Studies.

Miller, E.J., and Lerman, S.R. 1979. "A Model of Retail Location, Scale and Intensity." *Environment and Planning A* 11:177–192.

Miller, E.J., and Lerman, S.R. 1981. "Disaggregate Modelling and Decisions of Retail Firms: A Case Study of Clothing Retailers." *Environment and Planning A* 13:729–746.

Mills, E.S. 1972. *Urban Economics.* Glenview, Ill.: Scott, Foresman and Company.

Musgrave, R.A. 1938. "The Voluntary Exchange Theory of Public Economy." *Quarterly Journal of Economics* 53 (February):213–237.

————. 1959. *The Theory of Public Finance.* New York: McGraw-Hill.

Muth, R. 1969. *Cities and Housing.* Chicago: University of Chicago Press.

Noto, N.A. 1977. "The Impact of the Local Public Sector on Residential Property Value." In *Proceedings of the 69th Conference on Taxation, 1976.* Columbus: National Tax Association-Tax Institute of America.

————. "The Effect of Property Tax Policies on Property Values and Rents." In *Tax Policy Roundtable Property Tax Papers Series No. TRP-7.* Cambridge, Mass.: Lincoln Institute of Land Policy.

Oates, W.E. 1969. "The Effects of Property Taxes and Local Public Spending on Property Values: An Empirical Study of Tax Capitalization and the Tiebout Hypothesis." *Journal of Political Economy* 77 (November-December):957–971.

———. 1973. "The Effects of Property Taxes and Local Public Spending on Property Values: A Reply and Yet Further Results." *Journal of Political Economy* 81 (July-August):1004–1008.

———. 1981. "On Local Finance and the Tiebout Model." *American Economic Review* 71 (May):93–98.

Ohta, M., and Griliches, Z. 1975. "Automobile Prices Revisited: Extensions of the Hedonic Hypothesis." In *Household Production and Consumption,* ed. N. Terleckyj. New York: National Bureau of Economic Research.

Peterson, G.E. 1972. "The Use of Capitalization Effects to 'Test' the Tiebout Hypothesis." Working Paper No. 1207-4, Urban Institute.

Polinsky, A.M., and Shavell, S. 1975. "The Air Pollution and Property Value Debate." *Review of Economics and Statistics* 57 (February): 106–110.

Polinsky, A.M., and Shavell, S. 1976. "Amenities and Property Values in a Model of an Urban Area." *Journal of Public Economics* 5 (January-February): 119–129.

Pollakowski, H.O. 1973*a*. "The Effects of Local Public Services on Residential Location Decisions: An Empirical Study for the San Francisco Bay Area." Ph.D. dissertation, Department of Economics, University of California, Berkeley.

———. 1973*b*. "The Effects of Property Taxes and Local Public Spending on Property Values: A Comment and Further Results." *Journal of Political Economy* 81 (July-August):994–1003.

———. 1977. "Sources of Systematic Error in the Assessment of Urban Residential Property." In National Tax Association—Tax Institute of America, *Proceedings of the 69th Conference on Taxation, 1976,* pp. 89–97. Columbus.

———. 1981. "Housing Tenure Choice in a Spatial Setting." Working paper, MIT-Harvard Joint Center for Urban Studies.

Quigley, J.M. 1976. "Housing Demand in the Short Run: An Analysis of Polytomous Choice." *Explorations in Economic Research* 3 (Winter): 76–102.

Quigley, J.M., and Weinberg, D. 1977. "Intra-Urban Residential Mobility: A Review and Synthesis." *International Regional Science Review* 2 (Fall):41–66.

Radner, R., and Miller, L.S. 1970. "Demand and Supply in U.S. Higher Education: A Progress Report." *American Economic Review* 60 (May):326–334.

Reschovsky, A. 1979. "Residential Choice and the Local Public Sector: An Alternative Test of the 'Tiebout Hypothesis'." *Journal of Urban Economics* 6 (October): 501–520.

Rosen, S. 1974. "Hedonic Prices and Implicit Markets: Product Differentiation in Pure Competition." *Journal of Political Economy* 82 (January-February):34–55.

Samuelson, P.A. 1954. "The Pure Theory of Public Expenditures." *Review of Economics and Statistics* 36 (November):387–389.

———. 1955. "Diagrammatic Exposition of a Pure Theory of Public Expenditures." *Review of Economics and Statistics* 37 (November): 350–356.

Segal, D. 1979. "A Quasi-Loglinear Model of Neighborhood Choice." In *The Economics of Neighborhood,* ed. D. Segal. New York: Academic Press.

Shelton, J.P. 1968. "The Cost of Renting Versus Owning a Home." *Land Economics* 44 (February):59–72.

Siegel, J. 1975. "Intrametropolitan Migration: A Simultaneous Model of Employment and Residential Location of White and Black Households." *Journal of Urban Economics* 2 (January):29–47.

Small, K.A. 1975. "Air Pollution and Property Values: Further Comment." *Review of Economics and Statistics* 57 (February):111–113.

Sonstelie, J.C., and Portney, P.R. 1980. "Gross Rents and Market Values: Testing the Implications of Tiebout's Hypothesis." *Journal of Urban Economics* 7 (January):102–118.

Straszheim, M.R. 1973. "Estimation of the Demand for Urban Housing Services from Household Interview Data." *Review of Economics and Statistics* 55 (February):1–8.

———. 1975. *An Econometric Analysis of the Urban Housing Market.* New York: National Bureau of Economic Research.

Tiebout, C.M. 1956. "A Pure Theory of Local Expenditures." *Journal of Political Economy* 64 (October):416–424.

Triplett, J. 1969. "Automobiles and Hedonic Quality Measurement." *Journal of Political Economy* 77:408–417.

Weinberg, D. 1979. "The Determinants of Intra-urban Household Mobility." *Regional Science and Urban Economics* 9 (May-August):219–246.

Weisbrod, G.E. 1978. "Determinants of Residential Location Demand: Implications for Transportation Policy." Master's thesis, Department of Civil Engineering, Massachusetts Institute of Technology.

Weisbrod, G.E.; Lerman, S.R.; and Ben-Akiva, M. 1980. "Tradeoffs in Residential Location Decisions: Transportation Versus other Factors." *Transport Policy and Decision Making* 1:13–26.

White, K. 1972. "Estimation of the Liquidity Trap with a Generalized Functional Form." *Econometrica* 40:193–199.

Williams, R. 1979. "A Logit Model of Demand for Neighborhood." In *The Economics of Neighborhood,* ed. D. Segal. New York: Academic Press.

Yinger, J. 1980. "Capitalization and the Theory of Local Public Finance." Discussion paper D80-7, Kennedy School of Government, Harvard University, July.

————. 1981. "Capitalization and the Median Voter." *American Economic Review* 71 (May):99–103.

Zarembka, P. 1968. "Functional Form in the Demand for Money." *Journal of the American Statistical Association* 63:502–511.

————. 1974. "Transformation of Variables in Econometrics." In *Frontiers of Econometrics,* ed. P. Zarembka. New York: Academic Press.

Index

About the Author

Henry O. Pollakowski is a research associate at the Joint Center for Urban Studies of MIT and Harvard University. He received the A.B. in economics from the University of Michigan and the M.A. and Ph.D. in economics from the University of California at Berkeley. He has taught at the University of Washington, and has held visiting teaching positions at Harvard University and the University of York (U.K.). His published work has dealt with urban housing markets and local public finance.